Memories of a Golden Time

Growing Up on A Farm in Iowa in the "50's"

by
Gene Rinderknecht, D. V. M.

authorHOUSE™

1663 LIBERTY DRIVE, SUITE 200
BLOOMINGTON, INDIANA 47403
(800) 839-8640
WWW.AUTHORHOUSE.COM

First published by AuthorHouse 11/29/05

ISBN: 1-4208-7795-X (sc)

Printed in the United States of America
Bloomington, Indiana

This book is printed on acid-free paper.

Table of Contents

Forward

This book is a collection of stories and events that occurred as I grew up on a farm in rural Iowa. The time is essentially from 1947 (my birth) to 1965 (the year I graduated from high school). This was a great period of time in our country. It followed immediately after World War II and there was a tremendous amount of pride in what our country had accomplished. The United States and its allies had essentially saved the world from ruthless dictators who were bent on ruling the world. The sacrifices made by our citizens during that time were incredible in terms of energy spent, devotion to country, and for many, the ultimate sacrifice of giving their life for what they believed in. When I look back on that era of our country, I feel extremely fortunate to have lived during that time. Life in rural America was simple, peaceful, and to me there was no better place to be than on a farm in Iowa.

The stories contained in these pages reflect different aspects of life during that time. The early chapters in this book deal with the state of technology at that time. There is also a description of the farm and my family members. The stories that follow these introductory chapters are not in chronological order but stories and activities that occurred around a particular theme such as a holiday, a season, or family gathering. One of my purposes in writing these memoirs is that my children and grandchildren will have a better appreciation of what my childhood was like and about their ancestors who preceded me. I hope I can present each story so that you will have a vivid picture in your mind of how life was during this "golden time" in my life.

I would like to acknowledge my brother, Roger, and my three sisters, Verna, Jolene, and Luanne. Each of them reviewed my original manuscript to insure the accuracy of the information and gave suggestions for additional content. They all rummaged through their old scrap books and found photos that I used in the book as well. They all were very supportive of my efforts to bring this book to the printing stage as well.

I would also to thank my wife, Sandi, for her patience with me as I prepared this book. I did not personally log the hours that were involved, but I know they were considerable. She also reviewed the manuscript and helped select the photos contained in the book. I hope you all enjoy reading it as much as I enjoyed putting all the pieces together to record this very important time of my life.

Farmstead in the early 1950's

Farm Home 1980's

Farm Home 2004

Scenery around farm creek

Scenery around the farm

Fanning mill to clean grains such as oats

Elevator - used to transport hay in barn or grain in grainery

Manure spreader-hauled manure from barns to fields

John Deer Tractor- some of our neighbors had these

The Setting

The Time

Before I go further, I should elaborate a little on the relative state of modernization at this time in rural America. In the 1930's the whole country was turned upside down by the Great Depression and especially rural America. In the 1940's America was focused on winning a war not developing its infrastructure. So, mechanization of farm work really began after World War II, it was a time to start building tractors and combines instead of jeeps, tanks, and aircraft. I was very small at the time, but I can still remember having draft horses on the farm and my father doing field work with them. My father did not own his first tractor until after World War II. When I was almost five years old, our family moved from a small rented farm near Dysart, Ia. to a farm which dad had purchased in 1949. It was 160 acres or ¼ of a square mile of farm ground, a nice sized farm for that time. There were three other families that inhabited that square mile or section (640 acres) at that time. It was not unusual at all for 3-4 families to live on a section of land and to be able to make a living from those 160 acres. In 1957, dad purchased the 160 acres that adjoined our farm on the north side. This gave us a total of 320 acres or exactly one half of a square mile of farm ground. At that time, that was a good sized farm, today many farms are 1000 acres or more.

We received our news from the radio and newspapers. Televisions had been invented, but our first TV, black and white of course, did not arrive until 1953, when I was six years old. We had telephones and I can remember my mom ringing up the operator to connect her to make a call. That was followed by dial phones, but we shared a "party" line with 7 other neighbors. This could be frustrating if you had a talkative neighbor waiting for the phone to become idle, but it also provided some interesting entertainment listening to the neighbor's phone conversations or wondering who was listening to your conversation. Although the phone was used, a lot of information was shared neighbor to neighbor face to face. It certainly was not unusual for neighbors to stop by just to visit. Local news was also spread at a variety of social functions, i.e. card clubs, church activities, school functions, beauty parlors, etc. Although, my father rarely frequented the local "watering" holes, the local pool hall was a wonderful place to learn what was going on around town. As with many small towns, gossip was fairly prevalent. I was always amazed to learn that many people knew a lot more about our business than we did.

Recording the events of the day was done by filing them away in your brain and passing them on to the next generation. Cameras were available, but used very infrequently, at least by our family. The pictures were in black and white and only on rare occasions would mom break out her brownie camera to take pictures. Unlike today, with digital cameras where hundreds of pictures are taken each year.

The Location

I was born in the town of Vinton in an old brick hospital located in the southeast portion of town. That old hospital became the Lutheran Home for the Aged, which was eventually razed and a single family home now sits on that site. As I mentioned earlier our family was living on a small rented farm near the town of Dysart. Since I was so young, I remember very little about our home and farm in Dysart. I remember the house being very small.

There was a large red barn that had two levels. It was situated on a small hill so you could get into the upper level via a driveway and the lower level was like a walk-out basement where we milked cows. There was several out buildings as well. There was one old tool shed where I liked to hang out and pretend I was a mechanic. I believe there was also a single car garage that was detached from the house. Fortunately, I was able to find several pictures from that time, which are included in the book. This will give you a little flavor of how things were even though I do not recall a great deal about that time in my life. Just before I turned five years old we moved to the farm near Vinton. Our farm was located 6 ¼ miles southeast of Vinton, Iowa, a county seat town of about 5,000 people. The farmstead consisted of the house, a large barn, a corn crib/granary, a machine shed, a hog house, chicken house, two smaller livestock barns, and an assortment of smaller storage buildings. All of these buildings were designed with a specific purpose in mind and also served as areas of adventure and play for our family and neighborhood kids.

Our Home

When dad purchased the farm, there was not any electricity in the house, nor was there any indoor plumbing, and there was no forced air furnace. Before we moved to that farm, dad had electricity, running water, and a forced air furnace installed, central air conditioning was almost unheard of at that time.

When we moved into this home, I thought that old farm house was magnificent. We believe the home was built around 1908-1910. Its foundation was large limestone blocks hewn from a local quarry. They were neatly placed on top of each other and held in place with hand mixed mortar. It was a large two story home with a large gabled roof. Any exposed floor joist or rafters revealed the large rough cut timber. You could definitely smell the wood in the basement and attic where the wood was exposed. The interior walls were covered with thick plaster applied to wooden lathe underneath. There were some cracks in the plaster here and there, but for the most part, the smooth walls were a testament to the sturdy foundation the house was built upon. There was little or no settling of the walls to crack the plaster.

Shortly after we moved into that home, we did some remodeling. Dad's brother Henry or Hank was a carpenter, so whenever dad needed any carpentry work we called on his brother Hank. Dad & Hank built a two car garage and attached it to the house with a "breeze way". You did not have to go outside to get into your car. The kitchen was redone, leaving a modern kitchen with solid birch cupboards, a small room for work clothes, and a small ½ bath to clean up before meals. It was probably the most modern farm home around after that remodeling project. The first floor of that old farm house also had a large dining room, living room, and the bedroom for my parents. The dining room was rarely used for its intended purpose, except for large family gatherings. It quickly became the TV/family room once that first TV arrived. The living room was reserved for special visits or a place where the adults could escape for a little private conversation. There was a large upright piano in the living room. My three sisters all learned to play the piano and all became accomplished pianists and organists.

A long enclosed narrow staircase led to the second floor. The new bathroom complete with sink, stool, and tub was at the top of the stairs. Down the hall were three bedrooms. The bedrooms were huge and each bedroom had a walk in closet, almost unheard of in that day. My older brother and I shared one room, my older sister had her room, and my two younger sisters shared a bedroom. Behind the bathroom was a storage area we affectionately called the "junk room". This was a great place to hide and snoop around in the boxes of stuff stored there.

Another small enclosed stairway led to the attic. Our house had a large gabled roof, which created quite a large room with areas as high as 10 feet above the attic floor. The roof had four gables and each gable had a window which faced a different direction, north, south, east, and west. Since our home was located on top of a small rolling hill, we had a commanding view of the surrounding countryside from each of the four windows. Our attic was used for a little storage, but more importantly it was a great place to escape with friends to play games and pretend we were rulers of an ancient castle.

Our farm home also had a basement. Some creaky wooden stairs led to this rather dark, damp, musty hole in the ground. The limestone blocks that formed the basement walls, always seemed to be a little damp and slimy. The basement was mainly a storage area for odds and ends. My mother had a fruit cellar down there as well, where the efforts of her summer canning projects were stored. There was ample room to store enough home grown produce to carry us through those long Iowa winters. There was one rather large room that we cleaned up and painted. We used it as a play room for the kids and it was large enough to accommodate a full sized ping pong table as well. It was a neat area to play in, have ping pong tournaments, especially during the winter. We also had a shower in the basement. This was mainly used in the summer to wash away all the accumulated dirt and sweat from working long hours in the fields. It was a little chilly down there in the winter to take showers. My mother also had her laundry equipment in the basement as well. She had a large Maytag wringer washing machine and clothes dryer.

Certainly, many memories were made inside the walls of that old farm house. Memories created with family members and memories created when friends came over to visit and play.

Just as many memories were formed outside in all the different buildings that made up the farmstead.

The Barn

The barn on our farm was built in the early 1900's. It was a very large two story barn. The ground level was built for livestock while the upper level was designed to hold hay and bedding for the animals. Barns built during this time were incredible buildings. The main support structures were solid oak beams hewn from native lumber. They were meticulously cut and fitted together like a giant interlocking puzzle. Wooden pegs would lock one beam in place with another. Once these huge frames were in place, the outer walls of the barn were covered with one foot wide, one inch thick boards that stretched from the ground to the eves, some 20 feet. The spaces between these boards were then covered with one inch "bats" to seal the walls. The roof was covered with cedar shingles that with time and aging had a character all of their own. Finally, at the very top in the middle of the roof was the cupola. The cupola was designed to let air circulate out of the barn. It was large enough to crawl into and you had a commanding view of the countryside as you peered out from its louvered sides.

When originally built, one side of the lower level was intended to house cattle, in particular dairy, and the other side was to house the draft or work horses. One enclosed box stall was on each side. These were intended for one or two animals and were used for cows when calving and for horses when foaling. They were also used to house sick animals that might need a little extra attention. Solid oak mangers were on both sides of the barn. They were used to feed the livestock grain and hay. Everything about the interior of the barn conveyed a picture sturdiness and strength. They were built to withstand the rigors of the strongest beasts on the inside to the cruel weather extremes on the outside.

The upper level of the barn or hay loft was a cavernous structure. Solid oak beams supported the side walls and roof. There was enough space in the loft to store all the hay and bedding (straw) for those long Iowa winters. Filling the loft in summer with hay and straw was hard work. The smell in the barn after fresh baled hay was stored away is indescribable and a smell that was intoxicating as well. The hay loft also offered many opportunities for play. Tunnels and caverns were built out of the bales. Loose straw was often piled up and used as landing pads after flying through the air on a rope swing. As the hay and straw were used, the hay loft floor became exposed. This area was then converted into a basketball court where some intense games of basketball were played. I don't recall that we ever had a "barn dance" in our hay loft, but I know other farm families did especially if they did not use the loft to store hay or straw. This was always short lived however, as the crop of hay and straw soon covered the floor of the hay loft. Many critters enjoyed the safe confines of the loft as well. Pigeons and sparrows often used the loft for evening quarters and built nests to rear their young. Raccoons also liked the safety of the loft and if given the chance would try to snare a pigeon or two for dinner. Of course, the barnyard cats loved the entire barn to rump, play, and raise their young. Every barn on every farm seemed to have its own style and even culture depending on its purpose and what animals inhabited its interior. Many barns became obsolete as their usefulness declined. It was sad to see many once proud symbols of the American farm fall into disrepair, deteriorate, and even razed to make way for more modern "pole barns" that were more functional in nature. At one time, they truly were the center of farm activity and played a major role in the farm culture.

The Silo

Right next to the barn was a concrete silo. I do not recall the exact dimensions of the silo, but I believe it was about 18 feet in diameter by 50 feet tall. The silo was not there when we first moved to the farm. It was actually built after we tore down the original barn and put up a more modern, more functional pole barn. It was actually a little sad the summer we tore down that grand old structure and replaced it with the pole barn. We actually used a lot of the lumber from the old barn to build the new pole barn. Certainly a lot of good times and memories occurred in that old barn. Any way, the silo stood on the north side of the pole barn and its main purpose was to store livestock feed. It was either made from corn or from the hay crop. Silage was the whole plant that was harvested and ground in the field, blown into large forage wagons, and then transported to the silo. At the silo, a large blower would blow the silage to the top of the silo through a long tube and then it would fall from the tube to the bottom of the silo. Dad did not own any silage harvesting equipment, but instead, hired some of our first cousins to do the work. They did a lot of this work and it was a means to supplement their farm income. They would arrive with tractors, harvesting equipment, wagons, and the silo blower. Once everything was in place, they would get to work. Their equipment was large and they worked fast. It would normally only take one day to fill that huge silo. Occasionally they would let the silage settle overnight and put another wagon load or two in the silo the next morning.

Once the silo was filled, you had to stay away from it, because of the gases produced by the corn or hay fermenting in the silo. Essentially, you had created a large "fruit" jar of corn silage or haylage. The crops ground and put in the silo were green and would spoil if they were not allowed to ferment in the silo. The top one or two feet of the silage would spoil, but that would create an air tight seal, so that the rest of the silage would not spoil. During the fermenting process, toxic gases were produced, that if inhaled could be fatal. From time to time, you would hear of a farmer getting into the silo too early and either getting very sick or losing his life. After the silage had properly fermented or cured, it could be used for animal feed. It was excellent feed for both beef and dairy cattle, but we used it primarily for the beef cattle.

Silos had been on farms a long time and prior to electricity, required a lot of work to get the silage back out of the silo. You had to climb a ladder in an enclosed shoot, crawl through a small opening, and then with a silage fork, dig up the silage and throw it down the shoot into a wagon. As you emptied the silo, you had a series of doors that had to be opened to throw the silage down the shoot. Eventually you made it to the bottom of the silo, but every pound of silage had to be dug out and removed by hand. When dad built our silo, he had an electric silage unloader installed. This machine was raised to the top of the silo before it was filled. Once the silo was full, it was lowered by a cable and sat on top of the silage. It had a series of augers that would dig up the silage, carry it to the middle of the unloader and then a blower would blow the silage over to the shoot where it fell into a wagon. It was very simple to fill your fodder wagon. You would just back it under the shoot, push a button to turn on the unloader, and the silage

15

would pour down the shoot into the wagon. From time to time, you would need to go up into the silo and make some adjustments. You would need to lower the unloader so it sat on the silage. You would also have to open the access doors as the silage level went down and adjust the discharge shoot to the lower openings. That was a minimal amount of work compared to climbing the shoot each day and digging it all up by hand. Dad had bought a fodder or silage wagon to unload the silage. The fodder wagon was pulled and powered by a tractor. It had a series of conveyers and augers that would unload the silage right into the feed bunks for the cattle. This was a job I did not mind doing. The cattle were usually waiting for the silage and it seemed to be a real treat for them. Silage was hot when it came out of the silo, due to the fermenting process. In the winter, steam would rise from the wagon as it filled and from the bunks as it was delivered to the cattle. I think the cows appreciated this "hot" meal even more in the winter time.

Our silo had an aluminum dome that protected the silage from rain and snow. I liked to crawl up the silo and onto the dome. Our farmstead was on a hill and being on top of the silo, you could see quite a bit of the countryside. Summer time was the best time, particularly in the evening. It was nice and cool up there, there usually was a gentle breeze, and it was a view few people had the opportunity to have. I am not sure I could crawl up there today; my fear of heights would probably make me freeze up about 20 feet off the ground.

The Granary/Corn Crib

Much of the summer was devoted to raising crops. In the early fifties, most farms raised a variety of crops such as corn, oats, soybeans, and hay. The hay and straw was stored in the barn, the grain crops had to be stored in a granary or corn crib. Our farm had one large granary that stored corn, oats, and soybeans. At that time corn was harvested as whole ears of corn and stored in one side of the granary. The walls were slatted so that the corn could dry out. When needed, the corn was removed and either ground, whole ears at a time, for cattle feed. Or, the whole ears were removed and run through a large machine called a "corn sheller" so that you would be left with just the kernels of corn. Pigs' and chickens' digestive systems could not handle the cob portion of the corn so it had to be shelled first and then ground. Grinding grains was essential so that the livestock could properly digest the ingredients contained inside the grain. Besides the main granary we also had other smaller corn cribs to hold the corn. Some years when we had a bumper crop, we had to build temporary corn cribs to house the extra corn we grew.

The other side of the granary contained four, large, wood enclosed, bins. These bins were used to hold the oats, soybeans, and the kernels of corn, after being processed by the corn sheller. These bins were great places to play in. In the hot summer, you could burrow down into the stored grains where the temperature was much cooler. They were also great places to build roads, mountains, and imaginary buildings and pretend you were a master architect of this small piece of territory. There were no "sandy beaches" in Iowa so the grain bins served as our place to build "sand castles" and other imaginary structures.

The corn crib portion of the granary was separated from the storage bins by an alley way. This permitted you to pull a wagon through the alley way and shovel grain from the bins into a wagon. The grain had to be scooped out of the bins by hand into a wagon. This was very hard work to say the least. Eventually, electric augers were used to move the grain from the bins to wagons. The corn crib and bins were filled from the outside of the building. A large elevator was used. Grain from the fields was dumped by wagons into the elevator. The elevator contained a number of flat scoops connected by chains that carried the grain to the top of the granary. The grain was then dumped into a shoot through a hole in the granary roof. The shoot then delivered the grain to the appropriate bin or to the corn crib side of the granary. More on this in the "harvest time" section.

The Hog House

This was another busy place. The hog house was the place where the baby pigs were born, raised, and sent off to market. Our hog house was built by dad and Hank after we moved to the farm. It consisted of several pens on each side of an alley way. The alley was used primarily to clean the hog house and haul away the accumulated manure from the pens on each side. During farrowing, when the mother pigs (sows) delivered their baby pigs, farrowing crates were placed in the alley. These crates allowed the sows to lie down and the baby pigs could be on either side of the sow without fear of having the sow lay on the baby pigs and crush them. After farrowing and the baby pigs were a little stronger, the sow and babies were moved to a pen of their own. Eventually the piglets were weaned and joined the ranks of the other piglets in larger pens. Our hog house was designed so that wooden panels that separated the smaller pens could be removed and larger pens were created. In the winter, the pigs stayed primarily in the hog house and only went outside to eliminate and eat grain. In the summer, they were often taken to a pasture where portable sheds offered shelter from the summer's heat and a place to sleep at night. They also loved to root around in the sod or wallow about in the puddles after a summer's rain.

The Chicken House

This was not one of my favorite places. This building housed the adult female chickens whose primary purpose was to lay eggs. The building usually smelled bad from the chickens themselves and from the manure they produced. There were several rows of "nests" where the chickens went into to lay their eggs. There were also the roosts, where the chickens spent the night and where they eliminated creating large piles of very smelly chicken manure. There were also some larger open areas where the chickens could gather socially and to eat and drink. Taking care of the chickens was pretty much my mom's job. She would gather the eggs twice a day, make sure they had food and water, and place straw in the nests so the birds would lay their eggs on a soft cushion, making sure the eggs would not break after the hens passed them. She would tend to nearly 300 hens year round. Needless to say we had more than enough eggs for our family every day. The surplus eggs were washed and placed in large cardboard boxes. A local company would come once a week and pick up those eggs or neighbors who did not have chickens would buy a few dozen now and then. That gave mom a little spending money. My dad liked to remind mom that those chickens were a pretty expensive hobby and in no way ever paid for all the grain they consumed or the labor involved in caring for them. That didn't bother mom though, every year, we got a fresh batch of baby chicks to start the process over once again.

Each spring, usually in March, mom would get about 400 baby chicks from a local hatchery. She would get about 100 roosters (males) and 300 pullets (females) that would become the next crop of laying hens. The roosters were eventually killed and frozen and placed on the family dining table once winter came. The baby chicks were placed in a small chicken coop called a brooder house. Because they were only 1-2 days old and because it was still cold out, the brooder house was heated with a small, fuel oil fired, space heater. It was always a lot of fun to help care for those baby chicks. They grew quickly however and before long they were allowed out of the friendly confines of the brooder house to explore the world around them. Most would return at night to the roosts inside the brooder house, however, some would roost in the hardwood trees in our small grove of trees. This was a good deal until the neighborhood raccoons discovered these roosting chickens were easy pickings for a midnight snack.

By summer's end, the roosters had all been butchered and in the family freezer. The pullets were now mature and able to lay eggs. Last year's crop of hens was shipped off to be slaughtered. My dad would like to kid how they would become that delicious Campbell chicken noodle soup. The new pullets replaced the old hens in the chicken house and the process would start all over again.

As I said earlier, my mom pretty well cared for the chickens. The kids would help gather the eggs and help with cleaning them from time to time. However, all that accumulated manure under the chicken roosts had to be carried out. There was no nastier job on the farm than scooping out that chicken manure. It had to be done by hand and there was usually lots of it. As you began to remove it and stirred it up from under the roosts, the odor became almost overwhelming. Ammonia fumes would rise up from the piles of manure; it would burn your eyes and make your nose run. Some how it seemed like that was a job reserved for my brother and me and we both hated it. It's no wonder I was not a big fan of having those chickens around. It would have been a lot easier just to get eggs from a fellow farmer or in the store.

The Machine Shed

This was a long building that housed all the various pieces of equipment on the farm. Our farm like most farms then had a main machine shed and other small buildings where the machinery was stored. My dad liked to have all of his equipment in a building, especially during the winter months. The buildings protected the equipment from snow and rain and thus rusting. They also protected the tractors from winter's cold. It was always much easier starting those tractors if they had been inside than if they sat out and were exposed directly to the cold and wind. Usually there was one area of a machine shed that was designated to be the farm shop. This area had all the tools and equipment needed to do routine repair and maintenance of the farm equipment. Dad was a firm believer in preventative maintenance of his equipment. His machinery was usually in excellent repair and this prevented costly breakdowns especially during harvest time. One summer my brother and I decided to really organize the farm shop. We built a sturdy workbench and got all the tools and equipment organized. When we got done, "everything had its place and everything was in its place" dad really liked what we had done, but dad was one who didn't like to put things back in their designated spots. My brother and I spent a lot of time going around after my dad and picking up the tools he used and just left them where he used them. I think many times he did this just to aggravate my brother and me.

Other Out Buildings

We had other buildings on our farm as well. Some were small open sheds that housed cows and pigs. We had a large poled building with a tin roof called a hay barracks. This protected the hay crop from rain and snow and it also had mangers around its perimeter to feed cattle right on the spot. There were a variety of small buildings as well that stored equipment and supplies but did not offer much for play or adventure.

Farmsteads during that time were like small cities that housed people and a variety of animals. At times the city was fairly quiet and at times it was a very busy, lively place. No two days were ever the same, which made living on a farm such an interesting experience.

Mom's parents - August & Elizabeth Krug

Mom's parents - August & Elizabeth Krug Mom (back row 2nd from left) & her family

Mom - Louise Krug @ H.S. Graduation

Dad's parents - Martin & Bertha Rinderknecht

Dad (back row far left) & his family

Dad - Raymond Rinderknecht @ H.S. Graduation

Dad & Mom ready for a date

Dad & Mom Wedding Picture June 1,1941

Luanne, Mom, Dad, Jolene, Gene, Roger, Verna

Gene, Verna, & Roger

Luanne & Jolene

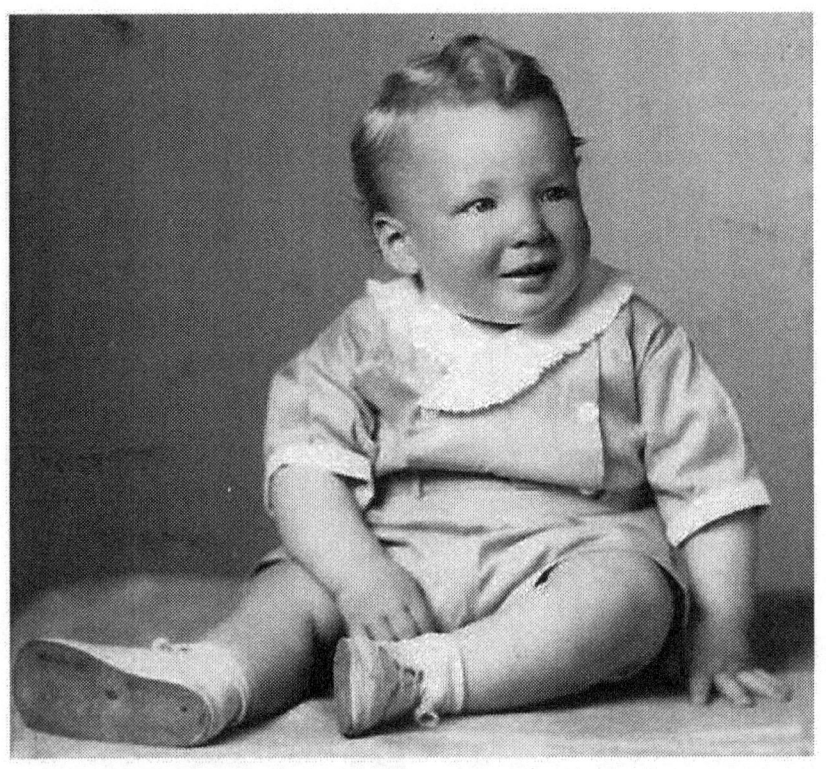

Gene's Baby Picture

Gene High School Graduation Spring 1965

Gene- birthday #4

In Vinton, Baby Jolene

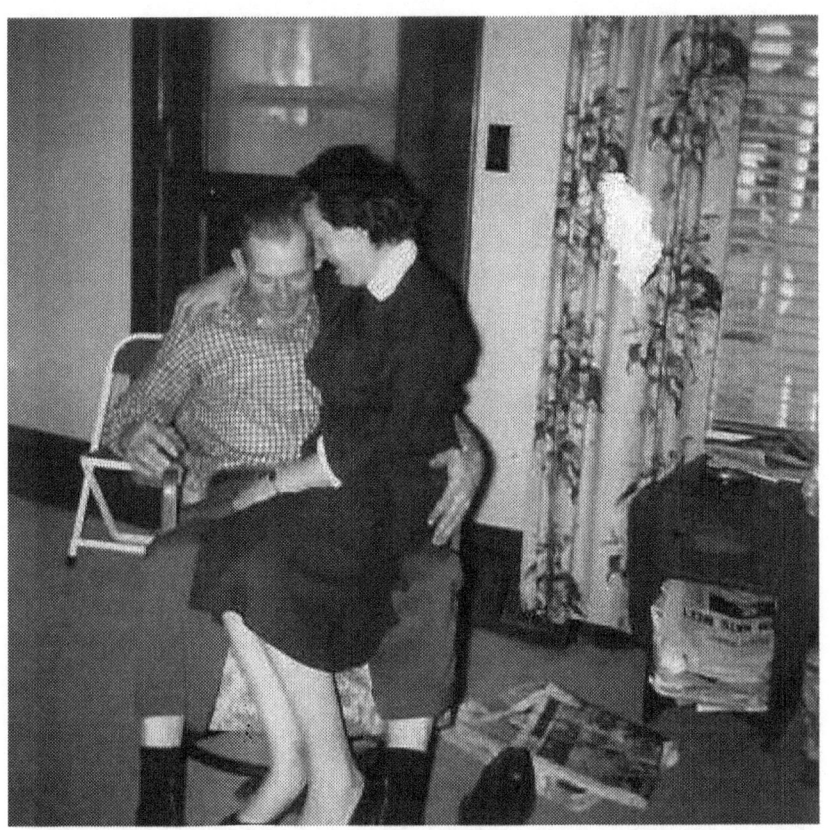

Mom & Dad

Mom & Dad

The Family

I grew up in a very structured family where roles for each family member were well defined. Those roles were not written out on some sacred scrolls and read aloud periodically so all would know what they were. Often times those roles were defined by long held family traditions and were more or less implied rather than stated. Men were men, women were women, husbands had duties and responsibilities, wives had duties and responsibilities, and finally children knew their boundaries and limitations as well. I was one of five children; having an older brother and sister and two younger sisters. I was that middle child with all the inherent advantages and disadvantages.

Dad

Dad was born in 1912 in Iowa on a small farm. His parents were of German descent and from a long line of farm families. He had a brother and four sisters, one of which died of a brain tumor. Dad was born during WW I, shortly after that the United States and for that matter the world was plunged into the Great Depression, and then WW II occurred. He grew up in a time when rural America had no electricity or indoor plumbing, and work on the farm was long and hard. Field work was done with draft horses and everything else was done by hand. Horses also provided transportation in his younger years, but were replaced quickly with the automobile. He used to talk about those early cars with a great deal of pride and admiration. His parents were staunch Lutherans besides being German. That translated into some very rigid guidelines, but also clearly defined the roles for men, women, and children. Men were supposed to be tough, they did the physical labor, and they were heads of the household. They were ultimately responsible for providing for the family. There was men's work and women's work. They tended to the farm work, made most of the family decisions, and acted as the supreme disciplinarian for law and order in the household. There was not much doubt who would measure out punishment if the children got out of line.

Dad enjoyed a good laugh or joke as much as anyone. He loved to joke and kid with anyone. He loved to play cards and was an excellent conversationalist. He had his serious side as well, but seemed to have a positive outlook about life no matter what came his way. He was a man of few words, yet you always knew where he stood. It was either black or white, there was no gray. Although he enjoyed conversation, talking about life with his children was not his thing. Whenever asked about life's more engaging questions, one or two words or a short sentence would be his answer rather than any long dissertation concerning the matter.

Dad saw his father lose a farm during the Great Depression. Having witnessed that and the abject poverty that so many faced during that time, left an indelible impression on his mind. The depression and its consequences affected how he conducted his financial affairs the rest of his life. He did not serve in the military during WW II as he had a young family and was also a farmer. Many of his close friends and relatives did serve, however, and some never returned. Like many young men of that time, he got hooked on Camel cigarettes. It was the thing to do then, and by the time he stopped smoking cigarettes the damage had been done. He never got lung cancer, but he did get emphysema which then resulted in congestive heart disease and his eventual demise.

As I said earlier, dad was rarely a complainer. He tried to be positive about all he did and I don't ever remember him regretting that he had done something or that he regretted not doing something. He took life as it was dealt to him and never looked back. He led life as an example to his family and his community. Dad died peacefully in his recliner watching a Bear's football game on a beautiful day in September. It was evident at his funeral how many lives he had touched by the number of people that were there and by the kind thoughts they shared about him. He was buried in Evergreen Cemetery in the same cemetery as his parents near the fields he grew up in and worked so hard to provide for his family.

Mom

Mom was born in 1918. Like dad, she was born on a farm and her parents were German Lutherans with a long history of a farm heritage. She had four brothers and three sisters. She grew up on a farm not far from where dad was growing up. Her father passed away at a young age before I was born. Grandpa Krug was a good business man and owned a full section of land (640 acres) when he died. The four boys eventually owned 160 acres while the girls ended up with no farm. Remember the time and the mentality. Boys were to be tough and do the work, girls were to be housewives and mothers, and therefore, they got little or nothing of his inheritance.

Dad was 28 and mom was 23 when they married. Farm couples were a definite partnership in those days. The men worked the fields and were head of the household. The women did the housework and were definitely the care givers to the family. Their families were close and knew one another. In fact, not too many years earlier, mom's brother married dad's sister. Sounds like incest, but it is not. So, we had double 1st cousins. I probably did not appreciate how hard my mother worked until I got married and found out how much work being "just a housewife" could be. There was 13 years difference between my oldest brother and my youngest sister. Raising 5 children is a challenge for anyone. Remember this occurred in a time before microwaves, automatic dishwashers, automatic clothes washers, and many other conveniences we take for granted.

She prepared three large meals each day, breakfast, dinner, and supper. When work crews were present during hay baling, corn shelling, or fall harvests, she would also prepare "lunches" and take them to the men working in the fields. She washed clothes in a wringer washer machine and when the weather was nice, hauled that laundry out to the clothes line to dry (the clothes just smell so much better after drying in the sun). She cleaned the house and washed the dishes, remember, this was women's work. She looked after her flock of chickens year round. In the summer, she had a huge garden that she planted, weeded, and harvested the fruits of her labor. There was nothing like that fresh garden produce. She also either canned or froze tons of fruits and vegetables to provide meals for us during those long winter days. She did not help out a lot with the field work or daily chores (we had two boys) but if we were short handed, she was always there to lend a hand. You could always count on Mom to help milk the cows or feed the livestock if someone was sick or laid up. The kids did help with various activities as we got older, like cleaning and gardening. However, as we got older and became involved in school activities and before we had our driver's license, mom became our taxi cab. We lived about 6 ½ miles from town and school. So, before school, after school, at night, on weekends, she was always there to haul us back and forth. I know some days she would make at least three trips a day into town and back. She seemed to find time to go to our activities, teach Sunday school, or be involved in some community project. I get worn out just listing all the things she was able to do.

When the kids all moved away from home, she kept busy with many civic activities and was very involved with church functions. In dad's later years, she tended to his various and assorted problems. After dad died, mom began to slowly slip away herself. Her reoccurring bouts of depression caused her and her family many sad moments. The woman created by this depression was so unlike the person we had known for so many years. Lots of different drugs and treatments seemed to work only temporarily and we all knew she was slowly drifting away. In the fall before she passed away, she was diagnosed with colon cancer. At 82 years of age and with increasing depression problems, everyone decided surgery was not an option.

I can recall going to visit mom at the University Hospitals where she was being cared for. We took a small entourage of my immediate family along with us. There were several of us including three of my children and three grand daughters. We met in a small lounge off the area where mom was staying. The grand daughters were young, some not even walking. It had been a long time since I think any of us had seen mom smile. However, as those little girls played on the floor and mom held the smaller ones on her lap, a smile finally appeared on her tired worn face. It was so precious, yet at the same time sad. These little girls that were so full of life would never get to know this woman that had lived her life to the fullest. That was in October and in early March of the following year, she passed away.

As with dad's funeral, there were lots of friends and family there. Once again a testament to the life she had led and how many lives she had touched in so many positive ways.

The Siblings

Roger: Roger was 5 years older than me. Back then, we shared a bedroom; there were just too many kids and not enough space to have a bedroom for every child. Roger had to pave the way for the rest of us and took his role as the first born son very seriously. He liked to do a lot of things especially sports. He headed off to college which was a big step as none of mom's siblings or dad's siblings had ever gone on to college. He graduated with a degree in agriculture education and taught agriculture at the high school level for several years. He soon became involved in the banking industry and made that his life's endeavor. He excelled in the banking industry and eventually retired. Roger married a home town girl named Rosen Anne. They had one girl and two boys and are blessed with several grandchildren.

Verna: Verna was three years older than me. She quickly became mom's best helper for all kinds of house activities and when the two younger sisters came along lent a big hand in bringing them up. She was an excellent student. I found that out as I followed her footsteps through our small school and her teachers reminded me of just how good a student she was. She was a very good musician. She played the clarinet in the high school band, learned to play the piano, and also played the pipe organ in our small church. She also enjoyed participating in high school plays and other more cultural activities. Verna also went off to college and became a registered nurse. Over the years she has used her nursing degree in many ways. She has practiced in some low income areas and in later years has been more involved with the academic side of the nursing profession. She met her husband Reg in college. They have a boy and a girl and two grand children.

Jolene: Jo was five years younger than me. She was quite a busy young lady and never short of energy. She was only a year and one half when her younger sister was born. They essentially grew up together and were very close. Jo was an excellent student as well. Following through school after me, the bar was not set real high. Jolene enjoyed music a great deal. She played in the band, learned to play the piano, and like her older sister, played the organ in our small church. Jo went off to college and got a degree in education. She has taught school faithfully to grade schoolers in a small town not too far from where she grew up. Jolene married someone from her hometown also. His name is Dan. They have three sons and at this writing, no grandchildren.

Luanne: Luanne was the youngest of the five children, 12 years younger than her oldest brother. As I said in the previous paragraph, Luanne and her sister Jolene were very close in age and consequently grew up together. They seemed to always play together and were best buddies. True to her older sisters, Luanne was a very good student and loved music. She played in the band, played the piano, and also played the church organ. Luanne became a teacher as well and has taught high school biology since she graduated from college. She met her husband Marc in college. They have one boy and one girl and currently no grandchildren.

Grandparents

Although my dad's father, Martin Rinderknecht, did not live with us, he was an integral part of the family. He and grandma Rinderknecht lived in Vinton in a small home. He liked to drive out to the farm and help in any way he could. In the spring he was there for the planting season, in the summer he would help with haying or putter around the farmstead, and in the fall, he would help with the harvest. He drove a 1949 Ford 2 door coupe. It was a three speed manual transmission mounted on the column. You could always hear him coming because he would slip the clutch and roar the engine as he glided into the farmstead. I think he did this so he could tell if the engine was running, since his hearing was not the best. In the early fifties, his health and mental state was fairly good, so Dad would let him do a lot of things. As time wore on, his memory was not good and he became frailer. He was small in stature and you could not imagine Raymond was his son; dad was six feet two inches tall while grandpa Rinderknecht was a mere five feet eight inches. He usually wore bib overalls and a faded blue work shirt. He almost always wore a hat and to see him without a pipe in his mouth was unusual. In fact, mom said I called him "Pipe" for a long time, because it seemed like a part of his body. Like dad, he was a man of few words. He liked to joke and kid like dad and always seemed to be upbeat. He was a farmer through and through. If land could not grow corn, it was of little or no value to him. I remember in the late sixties as the United States was getting close to landing on the moon he remarked to me; "Gener, I don't know why they want to go there, you can't grow any corn on the moon." As the years rolled on, his memory and physical abilities declined. He would often times repeat a story that he had told only minutes before. He quit coming to the farm as it was no longer safe for him to drive his car or operate farm equipment. I eventually got that 49 Ford and it became my "beating around" car. It was a pretty sweet machine, but not exactly a car the women were waiting in line to ride in. After he quit coming to the farm, he looked forward to our visits on Sunday after church.

He and I would usually visit and he would tell his usual run of stories.

One Sunday he told me he had something for me and disappeared into his bedroom. He emerged shortly with something in his right hand. He said, "I'm probably not going to be around much longer and want you to have this" as he placed it in my hand. It was his gold pocket watch that he had received from his dad when he was confirmed. I had seen this watch only once or twice before and actually forgotten that he had it. It still kept time, but the thin glass crystal covering the face was gone. Later on I had the crystal replaced and it became a cherished possession of mine. When I had my own veterinary clinic, I kept it in the top drawer of my desk. I would bring it out from time to admire it and remember the man who gave it to me. Unfortunately, it was stolen from my desk by an unscrupulous drug salesman. I am pretty sure who did it, but I could not prove it conclusively, and it has never been returned to me. It saddens me every time I think of it, the story connected to it, and the man who gave it to me.

Grandpa Rinderknecht was eventually admitted to a nursing home, which he thoroughly resented and detested. He died shortly after he entered the home. Unfortunately, I was in Georgia visiting my sister when he passed on and was unable to return for the funeral. That is one of life's regrets you wished you could do over, but impossible to do.

Grandma Rinderknecht (Bertha) rarely ventured out of her home. She had very serious problems with her legs. Most of the time she sat in her chair and barked orders to Martin. When she did get up and around she used a walker and every step seemed to be a struggle. Despite her disabled state, she always seemed cheerful. She enjoyed talking to the grand kids and would joke and kid with us. I think her favorite pastime was yelling at Martin and I think his favorite pastime was thinking up ways to aggravate her. He was hard of hearing, but I think it was very selective at times. As I said earlier, Martin seemed to always have a pipe in his hand or his mouth. He was never too careful with it either as he would either be spilling pipe tobacco on the floor or ashes from the pipe.

Bertha would chastise him continuously about this untidy habit. Since Bertha could not get around very well, she relied on Martin to do things for her or fetch things that she needed. Once again, her orders were given loudly to make sure he heard her. At times, Martin would go to the kitchen to get something for her and would conveniently forget to come back. This of course would bring more loud screams from Bertha and eventually he would return. In the summer time, when the windows were open, I am sure most of the neighbors could tell what was going on in their home. Bertha's loud voice would easily reverberate up and down the block as she told Martin what to do.

Martin proceeded Bertha in death at the nursing home. Bertha also entered the nursing home as her inability to get around the house became a safety issue. She seemed to enjoy it, as many of her friends and relatives were there. I believe her health actually improved during her stay since she lost some weight, had three good meals a day, and participated in some physical therapy to strengthen her arthritic legs. She died peacefully in her sleep one evening and was laid to rest next to Martin. Although I have some pictures with her and my children, they were far too young to remember their great grandmother.

Mom's parents were August and Elizabeth (Lizzie) Krug. My middle name is August after grandpa Krug. As stated earlier, he died before I was born and Roger and Verna were not very old when he passed away. Needless to say, I knew little about him and just heard bits and pieces of his life as I grew up. I am sure he was a shrewd business person because he was able to accumulate a fair amount of farm land before he died. I also came to realize he had strong beliefs concerning what men should be and do and what women should be and do.

Grandma Elizabeth lived alone in her home in Atkins, Iowa. Six of mom's siblings lived within a few miles of her, we probably lived about 10 miles away. There was probably not a day passed, that one of them did not pop in to visit with her. We would visit with her once a month or so and during family reunions. She was able to take care of herself, but it seemed whenever we visited her, she was just sitting in her rocking chair. She seemed to be a very quiet lady and it seemed whenever we were at her home she would visit with mom and dad. I think because we saw her so infrequently compared to the rest of her family, I never really got close to her. Once again, this is one of life's regrets, but nothing can be done to change the past. Elizabeth lived to be in her 80's and quietly passed away. I don't believe she ever entered a nursing home, but lived out her days at home with her immediate family caring for her.

Mom & Baby Gene

Dad, Verna, & Gene - Summer 1948

Gene In Verna's Baby Buggy

Rog, Verna, & Gene in the old red wagon -1948

Gene with his Trike

Rog & Verna going to school - Gene

A Typical Day on the Farm

Although every day on the farm was different, there was a normal day-to-day routine that was done to insure that the work did get done. There were those daily chores that had to be accomplished no matter what time of year or what other farm activity, such as planting or harvesting, was going on. My dad was one who believed in diversifying his income base. We raised hogs, we had feeder cattle, mom had her chickens, and we had a small dairy herd. We milked about 18-22 dairy cows and that was a chore that had to be done twice a day, seven days a week, 365 days a year. Dad also diversified his crops as well. We raised corn, soybeans, oats, and legume crops for making hay.

Activity on the farm started early. Dad would holler up the stairs to my bedroom between 5 to 5:30 AM every morning. It was usually a good idea to roll out of bed with his first call. If he did not hear your feet hitting the floor within a few minutes, he would give a second shout and then head up the stairs to see why you were still in bed. I would quickly dress and head down stairs. In the winter, it was very chilly in our bedroom, so you would throw on some extra clothes and hurry down the steps.

Getting the cows milked was the first order of business. When I first started to help milk the cows, we milked them in the big barn on our farmstead. After dad purchased the farm to the north of us, we moved the milking operation to that barn because it was more conducive to milking cows. We would hop in the pickup truck and make the short ½ mile drive up the road to the dairy barn. Dad liked to listen to the farm news, so when you turned the barn lights on, the radio came on as well. He always had it tuned to WMT, 600 AM, out of Cedar Rapids, Ia. They gave the livestock and grain market reports, weather, and farm related events. When my brother and I milked the cows by ourselves, we would usually switch the station to one that would play a little rock and roll music. Dad was convinced that rock and roll music was not very soothing to the cows, however.

An interesting story happened one Saturday when dad and I were milking the cows. For some unknown reason WMT always broadcast the Metropolitan Opera on Saturday afternoons. I am not sure why dad did not switch the station as neither one of us liked opera music in the dairy barn. Any way, one afternoon there was a guy and a gal singing their hearts out. One would call out to the other and then back and forth for several minutes. Dad was shaking his head trying to figure out what they were saying. He looked at me and said "I think I have this opera stuff figured out" I said, "Really, what are they doing?" Dad replied, "I believe the woman has a piece of barbed wire caught in her ass and the man is trying to pull it out!!!" I could not stop laughing and that is one of my favorite stories of all time. I think of it almost every time the word opera is mentioned. To this day, I do not enjoy opera either. I don't think I could sit through an opera without thinking of dad's interpretation of it and be able to control my laughter. We also continued to listen to the opera every Saturday, but dad did not come up with any more enlightening interpretations.

Through spring, summer and fall, the cows were usually out in the pasture. Depending on the time of year, it was often very dark when you headed out to find them. Although they had acres to roam in, there was usually one area of the field where the cows like to bed down for the night. Sometimes they would be close to the barn, so a quick jog out with the farm dog would quickly bring them to the milking barn. Sometimes they would decide to be at the far end of the pasture so I would hop in the old pickup truck and cruise out to get them. If on the odd occasion we were running a little late, the cows might even be at the barn door waiting to get in. Wanting a little relief from their milk distended udders and the fact they got some delicious grain with each milking prompted them to be waiting for us.

Our barn would only accommodate 10 cows at a time to be milked. So the whole group was placed in a holding pen. They were not milked in random order, but there was the first group of ten and then the second group. Each cow also had its designated stanchion as well. So, they knew who was going to be first and they knew exactly which stanchion they needed to be in. After they were in the barn the stanchions were secured so that some timid cow could not decide to exit before it was her turn to be milked.

Each cow was fed a grain ration according to her size and needs. They all seemed to be most appreciative as you poured out their ration in front of them. The next order of business was to spray them if flies were present; this was especially true in the summer. They seemed to appreciate us getting rid of those pesky flies as well.

For a short time, they could relax, have a good meal, not swat flies with their tail, and be relieved of all that milk that had accumulated in their udders over the last twelve hours. When I first started milking the cows, I was only ten years old, and the cows were milked by hand. Shortly after that, though, we did get milking machines. What a difference that made.

Once all the preliminaries were done, the cows were ready to be milked. Their teats and udders were cleaned with a soapy disinfectant and then dried. The milking machines were then applied and those bulging udders were drained. The actual milking process took less than 3 minutes per cow. We had three machines and as each cow was drained, we quickly moved onto the next cow. When the first group of 10 was done, the second group was moved in and the process was repeated. Prior to the milking machines, each cow was milked by hand and the milk was gathered in large stainless steel buckets. Every now and then a nervous cow would dance around and her dirty hoof would end up in the bucket and all the milk would be ruined. As these buckets were filled they would be set behind the cows. Once in a great while a hungry barn cat would try to drink out of the bucket or a smaller cat would try to balance on the rim of the bucket and would fall in the bucket. Once again, ruining all that fresh drawn milk. Whether milked by hand or by the machines, the milk we collected was strained through a filter and placed in a large stainless steel refrigerated tank. Usually twice a week a large tank truck would come and pick up the milk and haul it to the dairy. Every two weeks, dad would get a nice check in the mail from the sale of the milk. He liked that a lot, because it was a constant stream of cash flow he could count on. Unlike selling crops or other livestock where you only got paid when your produce went to market.

When winter weather came, the cows were no longer allowed to go to pasture. They were confined to the barnyard and had large "loafing" sheds to go in to escape the cold. When really cold weather set in (below zero), we would often times leave a group of 10 cows stanchioned in the milking barn. They stayed warmer and it also helped keep the milking area warmer as well. These barns were not heated and only those thin wooden walls protected you from the howling winter winds. It was very hard to get up on those cold mornings to do the milking. It was neat however to come in the milking barn when the cows were kept there overnight. I can remember turning on the lights and seeing the "steam" rising up from their bodies and their exhaled air. The barn cats also seemed to enjoy it as well and some even found cows that would allow them to sleep on their warm backs. The cows seemed to appreciate the extra comfort and seemed a bit reluctant to head back outside after they were milked.

Milking cows was not without hazards. Our barns were neither air conditioned nor heated. There was nothing quite like a hot summer day with temperatures in the 90's and that much humidity maneuvering between cows that were 100 degrees. A large fan at one end of the barn and a summer breeze made the task a little more tolerable. It was not unusual to be hit in the face with a madly swinging tail trying to chase away a biting fly. You felt fortunate if the tail was not caked with manure as it hit you. Some cows did not always appreciate your efforts as well, so being kicked or stepped on was always possible. Having your toes stepped on by a 1000 pound plus critter is never pleasant, but especially in the winter when your toes were nearly frozen stiff was even worse. The full extent of the pain was not often felt until several hours later when your toes began to unthaw.

In the winter after the cows were milked, you had to make sure there was hay in the manger for them to consume. That done, we headed back to the house for breakfast. I always enjoyed our big farm breakfasts, but especially in the winter. Coming in out of the cold to those delicious smells and hot food was very special. As soon as you entered the back door, the smell of fresh brewed coffee, bacon or sausage, and fresh baked cinnamon rolls elevated your appetite even more. A typical breakfast was orange juice, eggs, meat (bacon, sausage, or ham), toast, and cereal (cold in the summer, oatmeal or malt o' meal in the winter. We ate potatoes at all of our other meals, so we rarely had them for breakfast. We did not always have fresh baked rolls, but when we did, mom made them from scratch and they were heavenly. Dad loved his coffee with cream, but I never acquired a taste for it until I went to college.

After breakfast a few more chores needed to be done. During the school year, I would hustle out after breakfast and tend to my 4-H projects, normally 2 or 3 steers I would show at the county fair. This was done in the summer as well, but once completed, field work and other jobs of summer were done. Dad usually went about the rest of the chores. He would make sure the feeder cattle had grain and hay; the hog feeders were checked to see if there was enough grain for the day; and a general inspection of the farmstead for minor problems. In winter, he also had to make sure all the watering facilities were free of ice. This usually meant checking each individual watering trough to make sure whatever type of heat that was used to keep it thawed was working properly. This was no easy task at times especially when temperatures reached 20 degrees below zero and wind chills were in the negative 40-50 degree range.

In the summer, many tasks had to be done. However, my dad liked schedules and he liked to stick to them as much as possible. It seemed no matter what we were doing, when 12 noon came, we stopped and went to the house for dinner. My mom appreciated the fact that he stayed to a schedule; she could plan her day with a great deal of certainty as well. The noon meal or dinner as we called it was huge. In the summer, you had no problem working off that big breakfast and by noon you were ready to chow down again. The noon meal consisted of potatoes, vegetables, breads, meat or chicken, and some wonderful homemade desserts, fresh pies or cakes, and usually with ice cream. The noon meal was usually completed by 12:30 and then it was nap time. My dad was a firm believer in the mid day nap. He was usually out like a light in a matter of minutes, but when 1 PM rolled around he was up ready to go for the afternoon. I liked this idea as well, but there were many days when I wished that nap could have been longer.

After our meal and nap, it was back to the fields or whatever activity was going on. Just as we routinely stopped at noon, we stopped our afternoon activity around 5 PM to milk the cows. Milking the cows was essentially a two person job; usually it was my brother and me. So, dad would often times continue working while we milked the cows. When that chore was completed though, we would all return to the house for the evening meal or supper.

Supper was like an instant replay of the noon meal. Lots of potatoes, vegetables, meats, and desserts were served. Dad was pretty much a meat and potatoes type of guy. Casseroles were rarely eaten at home and usually showed up at social gatherings and family reunions. Supper was usually done at a less hurried pace than dinner, we did not have to get back to the fields. It was a time when the seven of us were all around the table and the days events were discussed. During the school year, what we did in school that day was a pretty standard question. When we ate, there was no radio on and after the TV arrived, it was never turned on during meals. Thinking back, that was a great rule.

During the school year, I would get home from school, change clothes and head out to do my evening chores. That consisted of taking care of the 4-H project and milking those beloved cows.

After dinner, and every meal, mom and my sisters did the dishes, again women's work. The men would retire to the TV room to let the large meal settle. If it was still nice out and there was work to be done, it was not unusual to head out and work until dark. During the hot summer months, everyone usually retired to the front yard. This was on the east side of the house and our large two story home cast a wide cool shadow on the grass. We would sit and just enjoy the cool of the evening. Neighbors would drive by and wave or would stop into visit. Our closest neighbors were at least a half mile away, but I think we knew everyone within miles of the farmstead. Farming communities were tight communities and neighbors spent time with each other and lasting friendships were built. You truly knew your neighbors.

In the summer, we kids would often entertain ourselves by catching fireflies and putting them in glass mason jars. Before it got dark, we might hit the softball a little or play a little badminton. Sometimes I would just lie on my back and look at the stars. In the country away from all the city lights, you could see stars by the millions. It was so relaxing. When the moon was full, it would illuminate the country side almost like daylight. You could see cattle peacefully grazing in the pastures on our rolling countryside. It was very quiet as well, no loud traffic, no jets roaring overhead, or someone's loud stereo violating the nighttime quiet. You could hear the crickets, an occasional cow bellow, or the clank of a lid on a self feeding hog feeder.

Despite that big supper, snacks were usually in order before bedtime. That might be fresh popped popcorn made in a skillet, another piece of pie or cake, or maybe some candy Mom would bring out of hiding as a treat. Bed time usually came before 10 PM, because at 5 AM we would be back up and headed for the barn to milk those cows.

My bedroom had an east facing window and my bed was next to that window. I loved going to sleep looking out that window, watching the moon, or the stars, or the occasional car that was driving down a road some distance from our house. In the winter, that same scene could be transformed by a snowfall or a landscape totally blanketed with snow. That peace and tranquility seemed to be shattered all too soon by dad's deep voice telling me it was time to get up and milk the cows.

Gene & a 1949 Ford

Our Family, Dad's Parents - ready for church

Dad, Rog, Verna, Gene & the 49 Ford

The whole family off to church

The Sunday Routine

Dad liked to stick to routines and Sunday was no different. Monday through Saturday (this was no day to relax) were work days, however Sunday was a little bit different. The cows had to be milked and the livestock needed to be tended to. Sunday was pretty much the Lord's Day and a day to relax and spend with family. Very unusual circumstances had to be in place to interrupt the Sunday ritual.

We would still rise early, milk the cows, do the chores, and have that big breakfast. After that, we got out our Sunday best and headed off to church. We attended a small Missouri synod Lutheran church in the town of Vinton. This church was started and built my dad's father, my grandfather, and his immediate family. It was a small wood frame building painted white. The walls were covered with wood siding that was interrupted periodically with stained glass windows. A wooden bell tower rose above the steeply pitched roof. The church bell was always rung to announce the start of worship service; I am sure much to the chagrin of the church neighbors. The inside of the church was fairly Spartan. The walls were plain white with their plain appearance broken only by the stained glass windows. The ceiling was open exposing the large oaken beams that supported the roof. The ceiling itself was oak wainscoting that was stained very dark. The pews were darkly stained solid oak as well with no seat cushions. The floors were wooden with badly worn carpet covering the center and side aisles. The floors would squeak as people entered the church. A large pipe organ was in front of the church, which when played by someone with musical talent could about blow you out of your pew.

The men all wore suits, white shirts, and ties. In the winter they wore heavy top coats and fedoras. The women wore their dresses and hats. Church was taken very seriously then. You entered church, usually sat in the same pew, and quietly waited for the service to begin. Visiting was a no-no and I think smiling and looking pleasant was frowned upon as well. Being Lutheran at that time meant you followed one of several liturgical services. These liturgies were difficult to sing and after singing them several times, the words just flowed out of your mouth with no real thought as to what you were saying. The hymns we sang also seemed way to somber for me. Many were written hundreds of years before my time and I could not see the relevance for the time I was living in. The hymns and liturgy were intended to prepare you for the sermon that day. Although the occasional sermon seemed to have a relevant message, most of the time, they would have made excellent material to aid insomniacs. The sermon was followed by prayers and a closing hymn. When you are young, time seems to go by slowly, sitting in that small church on Sunday seemed to make time stand still.

After church the youngsters 4-14 years attended Sunday school. When I attended, I had to admit I enjoyed the classes. Most of my class was school chums, neighborhood kids, or cousins. It was more like a small social gathering. We did learn about some very interesting bible stories and I felt I took away some important lessons from them.

After the church activities, we would drive down to the local drug store. We would pick up a Sunday paper for ourselves and for my grandparents (my dad's parents). In that time, there were few if any businesses open on Sunday, it was truly a day for all to relax and be with family. Dad's parents, Martin & Bertha, did not live too far from the church and we always stopped by to pay them a visit and give them the Sunday paper. As I said earlier Bertha would usually be screaming orders to Martin when we arrived. Martin loved to visit with me and he would always tell me stories of his farm experiences. As the years rolled on and his memory faded, the stories did not change, but often times were repeated over and over. I believe one of the reasons he liked to visit with me so much is that it gave him a break from Bertha for an hour or so.

After the visit with the grandparents, we would head home for Sunday dinner. Mom would often times prepare a meal that could be baked in the oven. She would set the timer on the oven so that when we arrived home it would be nearly done. When you came in the house the smell of baked ham or chicken, scalloped potatoes, and baked beans permeated the air. This was a big meal and as with most all of the meals mom prepared it was topped off with homemade pie or cake. A nap was usually in store after such a big meal.

The afternoons on Sunday were pretty leisurely. Friends or relatives might stop by or we would go visit them. Dad would like to just hop in the car and drive around the countryside in the summer. He would like to see how his crops compared to the neighbors. He always prided himself in having well manicured crops with very few weeds. He almost had an obsession of ridding his fields of weeds. In our drives, if he saw someone he knew sitting in the front yard, we would stop in and chat for a bit. Often times our drives would end up at my mom's mother's home, Grandma Krug. As I mentioned earlier, she became a widow before I was born. Grandma Krug was a small, hunched over lady. Although she was fairly mobile, I remember her most, just sitting in her rocking chair. I just never seemed to know her that well. I only saw her once a month and usually she and my parents would visit. She was a kind lady and I did feel sorry for her living all alone in her small home. Grandma Krug would never allow us to leave her home without giving us some ice cream, pie, cake, or some other goodie. I guess she thought her daughter, my mom, did not know how to make desserts.

No matter what we did on those Sunday afternoons, it was usually done as a family. Of course the cows were always waiting for us and it always gave dad a good excuse to move on if things got a little boring. Sunday evenings were quiet as well. TV became the evening's entertainment before we turned in and another week of work on the farm began.

Roger, Vema, & Gene -Winter 1949

Gene on an F-20 Tractor

Gene in Farm tool shed

Gene grinding something

Lu, Gene & Jo on the yard swing

Gene & Dad after an Iowa Blizzard

A wagon like this was used to sow oats

An old two bottom plow

Farmall M Tractor - similar to one we had

Modern combine

Pull type corn picker

Two row corn planter

Field Disk for preparing fields to plant

Hay baler - used to make hay in summer

Hay mower - used to cut hay

Hay rake - used to make hay winrows

Hay Rake - used to haul hay

The Seasons

Although many activities occurred on the farm, probably there was nothing more significant than what happened during the four seasons of the year. Raising crops was a major event on the farm. We raised several crops. Corn was raised primarily to feed the livestock and the excess was sold. Soy beans were pretty much a cash crop and were sold in the market place. Oats was a rather small crop in terms of the amount of acres used. It was usually fed in some form to the livestock since it had a very low cash value. A secondary crop of oats was the straw from the oat shafts which was baled and used for livestock bedding. Hay crops were also raised. This was primarily alfalfa and clover. You could normally get two complete hay crops from the same field and in a good year you might even get a third.

Dad was pretty much a believer in rotating crops, that is, alternating crops every year in the same field. Oats was followed by hay, which was followed by corn, and that was followed by soy beans. Some fields were set aside to be used for pasture for the livestock. As land became more and more valuable, crops such as oats, hay, and pasture nearly disappeared, since they could not produce the income like corn or soy beans.

Spring

I always enjoyed spring and in fact eagerly looked forward to it. After the cold winters and being confined to the indoors for most of that time, it was nice to be able to get out and not have to wear mountains of clothes to keep warm.

Spring of course was the season of planting when all the crops you hoped to harvest in the months ahead had to be planted. The spring planting activity would usually start in late March or early April. The planting season started when the weather permitted. The snow had to be gone and the frost out of the ground before the land could be tilled. The ground could not be too wet as well. Many things had to come together to make conditions ideal. I am not sure if conditions were ever ideal, but year after year the ground was tilled and the crops were planted and rarely was there ever a total crop failure.

In the early fifties, mechanization of the field work was fairly universal. The equipment though modern in that time period, would seem extremely crude today. Tractors of that era were man killers to say the least. There was no power steering, no power brakes, no automatic transmissions, and no comfort controlled cabs that protected the operator from the elements. You would sit on a very uncomfortable seat over the rear wheels. Guiding those tractors through the fields took a great deal of brute strength. They had no suspension so, at times as you rolled over the fields you felt more like you were on a bucking bronco. If you spent most of the day riding a tractor, by days end you felt like you had really been run through the mill. Chiropractors made a good living adjusting contorted bodies back into alignment. Tractors were not the huge machines that farmers drive today. Consequently, the equipment they could handle was small. For the field to be properly prepared, you had to go back and forth many times to accomplish your task. This continual back and forth activity could be extremely boring and you wondered if you would ever get your job done. What can be accomplished in hours with today's modern equipment took days to accomplish then. Farmers like my dad however, remembered how long it took to do the same work with a team of horses. They were thrilled to sit on those tractors and watch how quickly they got things done. As dad would say I would much rather sit on that tractor seat and bounce around, then follow a team of horses down the field and smell horse farts all day.

Oats was the first crop that was planted and it typically was planted in a field that was corn the year before. The corn stalks that were now dry and brittle had to be broken up further before the oats could be planted. This was accomplished by using a machine called a disk. The disk was pulled by a tractor that broke up the corn stalks and stirred up the soil to make it ready for the oats. After this process, a "drag" was used to smooth over the soil. With the ground now prepared, the oats were planted. We used an "end gate seeder" in the back of a wagon to do this. It had a large hopper where the seed oats were shoveled in. As the wagon moved over the ground two fan like devices caught the seed from the hopper and scattered it over the ground. It was a rather crude device in many ways, but somehow there always seemed to be lots of young plants emerge from the soil and produce a nice crop of oats. Next years' hay crop was planted at the same time. The tiny seeds were placed in a smaller hopper and went out with the oat seeds. After the oats was harvested, the hay crop would grow up through the oat stubble and the following year produce some very good hay.

Corn was the next crop to be planted. By this time, it was usually late April or early May. Most of the farmers liked to plant corn in early May. There was usually no more risk of frost by then. This was very important since frost could seriously stunt or kill the very tender emerging corn plants. Planting early in May also assured the corn would have time to grow and mature before the fall frosts arrived, which could also damage the corn plants.

During that era, the fields designated for corn took a lot of preparation. The fields had to be plowed. A plow would essentially take a slab of soil and invert it 180 degrees. This process allowed fresh black top soil to be exposed and the surface debris was completely covered. Plowing the fields was done sometimes in the fall of the year after the harvest was completed or in the spring right before you wanted to plant corn. Fall plowing saved you time in the spring, but that nice black top soil was exposed to the elements all winter long and erosion could occur from wind and rain. Even in the spring, excessive rains could cause water erosion. I can recall after some very heavy rain, the local creeks, streams, and rivers running brown/black with that precious top soil. If it was too dry, the strong prevailing spring winds could cause serious wind erosion. I remember during the dry times, when the top soil was parched, and the wind was blowing how the sky would become nearly black as all the top soil became air born. Needless to say, traditional plowing of the fields came under attack. It certainly was an environmental concern and most farmers realized that if they continued to use this traditional method of field preparation that someday, their topsoil, and thus their source of making a living would be gone. Eventually, newer methods of field tilling came on the scene which were much more environmentally sensitive and at the same time preserved the topsoil.

Once the fields were plowed, the ground had to be further worked so the seeds of corn could be planted. There was a feeling amongst most farmers then that the ground had to be well worked and smooth before the corn could be planted. Thus, it might take several passes with disks, drags, and other equipment before the ground was perfect. Corn was planted with a machine interestingly enough called a "corn planter".

The early corn planters planted only two rows of corn. Corn rows at that time were usually 40 inches wide. This was fairly standard at this time and the reason for this width was that anything narrower would not allow a horse to walk down between the rows of corn. You can imagine how long it would take to plant a field of corn when you were covering 40 inches at a time and fields were often ¼ or ½ mile in length. I do remember dad planting corn with a two row planter. However, it wasn't long before he purchased a four row planter. Imagine, covering twice as much ground as before! You could plant your fields in half the time.

Each planter was composed of a series of hoppers for each row of corn to be planted. One hopper was for the seed corn and one hopper was for a "starter" fertilizer. Later on, additional hoppers were added for applying weed killers, to get a jump on early weeds, and another hopper for insecticide, to kill those nasty bugs that liked to attack the tender corn plants. It was a major responsibility to plant the corn and one that dad usually did himself. You had to drive straight across the fields so when the plants emerged, the corn rows would be straight as an arrow. What would the neighbors think if the rows were crooked or wavy? Also, you had to make sure all of the hoppers stayed full. It would be very embarrassing to let a seed corn hopper run dry and have a barren row from lack of seed. You also had to make sure the planter was working OK. Sometimes there would be a malfunction of the planter. Seed, or fertilizer, or weed killer, or insecticide might not be placed in the ground. As I said earlier, this was a big responsibility and dad felt he was the one to do this job. My brother and I agreed and were usually happy to let dad do this job, it was also very boring as well.

Eventually planters got even bigger and as people realized horses did not need to go down the rows, the width of the rows became narrower. I think today, there are 16 row corn planters and the row width is 30 inches.

Once in the ground, it was up to Mother Nature to furnish rain and lots of sunshine to insure there was a bumper crop in the fall.

The last crop to be planted was soybeans. Field preparation for this crop was similar to corn. Most farmers liked to have their soybeans planted by the 1st of June. This usually allowed enough time for the crop to grow and mature before the fall frost set in. Soybeans were planted with the corn planter. The planter had to be modified slightly to accommodate the soy seeds. Most of the time, it was just the soy seeds that were planted. Starter fertilizer, weed killers, and insecticides were rarely applied at the time of planting.

Once the crops were planted, there was always a collective sigh of relief. After all, you could not hope for a good harvest until the crops were in the ground. There always seemed to be competition amongst the neighboring farmers to see who got the crops in first. It was just one of those unstated events. You would not call up your neighbor and say "I beat you", but there was always a sense of pride and accomplishment if you finished first. Because of the competition and because Mother Nature would not always cooperate, you had to work the fields when conditions permitted. It would not be unusual at all to be in the fields early in the morning just as the sun was coming up. Or, it would not be unusual to be in the fields late at night. Tractors had headlamps to light your way. Often times you could look out over the darkened rolling hills and see the glimmer of tractor lights plying their way back and forth to get the work done. Field work could involve 16-18 hours a day if you were behind schedule, the weather permitted you to work that long, or you just wanted to put in a long day. Although getting the crops in was very important and seemed to be the focus of attention during April and May, the regular day to day duties and chores had to be done. Cows had to be milked, livestock feed had to be prepared, and livestock had to be fed and tended to. It seems I always ended up milking the cows while my brother or dad worked in the fields. That was not always a bad thing because as I stated earlier, field work could be very boring and also very rough physically.

If the weather was right, however, working at night was actually rather peaceful. It was just you alone on that tractor and the rest of the world did not matter. I can remember sitting on that tractor when it was dark. The tractor would make a loud droning noise as it labored to pull some piece of equipment across the fields. You could see millions of stars if the moon was dim or if the moon was bright, you could look out over the peaceful rolling hills. You could also see the dim lights of other tractors in your neighbors' fields going back and forth. I think there was competition to see who might work the latest. Since it was spring and I was still in school, I rarely stayed out past 9 PM. I may have had some school work to do and for sure I had to get up early and milk the cows. Some neighbors would work all night long just to get their work done. I don't ever recall us ever doing that. My dad did have a lot of common sense.

One activity that was usually done in the spring but could also stretch over summer and fall was hauling manure. When you have pigs, cattle, and chickens, they all produce lots of manure. In the winter, it would be difficult to get rid of the manure, because it would often times freeze to the ground or wherever the animal dropped it. Also, because the weather was often times so bitterly cold, you just did not want to be outside. The animal manure was often times mixed with the straw bedding. This combination was excellent natural fertilizer. So, if you could get the manure hauled out onto the fields in the early spring, you could reduce some of your regular fertilizer costs as well.

Getting rid of the manure was accomplished in two ways. In the chicken house and hog house, the areas were just too small to get a tractor and end loader in the building, so it had to be loaded on to the manure spreader by hand. I will say a quick word about manure spreaders. These were wagon like devices that had conveyer chains in the bottom of the spreader and in the back were a series of rotating tines that would gather the manure and fling it out of the spreader. You would load these manure spreaders full and drive to the fields. Once you got to your desired location you would engage the manure spreader. The conveyer chains would pull the manure to the back of the wagon and the rotating tines would then distribute the manure onto the field. It was always a good idea not to drive down wind from the spreader. On a windy day, a stiff breeze just might take that air borne manure and pelt you in the back...

Any way, if you had to load the spreader by hand, this was a lot of work. You might have to use a scoop shovel to throw it in the spreader. Often times you would have to use a pitch fork to dig up the manure that was mixed with the straw. Not only was the manure heavy, but the straw often times made it difficult to dig it up. Although never a fun job, digging up the chicken manure under the roosts was the worst. Compacted chicken manure was very heavy, the ammonia smell could be overwhelming, and you usually had to carry it a fair distance before you could fling it in the manure spreader.

Cleaning up after the cattle was a little easier. They often spent their time in barns, loafing sheds, or on large mounds outside that could be accessed with a tractor and end loader. These end loaders were mounted on regular tractors when needed. This was a time before self contained end loaders like Bobcats were around. The tractor would push the end loader into a pile of manure. Hydraulic cylinders would then lift the bucket full of manure into the air and then dump it into the manure spreader. Once loaded it was hauled to the fields. This was certainly a much easier job then by hand. However, after many months of waste accumulation, the piles of manure could be quite high and it might take several days to get rid of all that waste.

Summer

According to the calendar, summer officially started in late June. However, on the farm summer started when the crops were all planted and the kids were out of school. That was usually the 1st of June. Once out of school for the summer, working on the farm became a full time job even for the kids. It didn't really matter how old you were, there was always some task you could do to contribute to the entire enterprise. The boys helped in the fields and tended the livestock, the girls helped with the garden and the household chores. Summer was not the time to be playing baseball, going to camp, or kicking back and relaxing. It was a time for lots of hard physical work.

Before I discuss the activities that occurred on our farm, I would like to talk about an activity that was at least unique to our immediate area. The Green Giant Company had a canning facility in the town of Vinton. They processed asparagus, peas, and sweet corn. Many of the local farmers raised these vegetables to sell to Green Giant. Interestingly, Green Giant brought in migrant workers every summer to harvest these three vegetables. These were Hispanic people, probably from Mexico, but most said they were from South Texas. Green Giant provided housing for these migrant workers in a small "camp" on the southeast corner of town very near the fairgrounds. It had no specific name as I recall, but everyone called it the "Mexican Camp". I never visited the camp, but we drove by it several times a week. It was not a very pretty place to say the least. It was just a series of long buildings that more resembled an army barracks. I also don't recall how many migrants lived there, but it seemed like there were a lot of folks crammed into some very tight quarters. The workers and their families stayed pretty much to themselves and only ventured into town to buy their basic necessities. Once in a while their hard earned money was spent at the local bars and some fights broke out. I don't think anyone was seriously injured.

I was always amazed at how hard these migrants worked. Early in the summer, they would pick the asparagus. They would move across the fields and pick each stalk by hand and put it in a big sack.. When the asparagus harvest was done, they continued with the peas and then the sweet corn. Mechanical "pickers" were used for the peas and corn, but none the less harvesting these crops took a lot of work on their part in the hot Iowa sun.

Some of the migrants would hire out to local farmers to make a little extra money. Most of the time they helped with hay baling. They would unload the wagons of hay or work in the hay mows stacking the bales away. They worked very hard for very little money, but seemed most appreciative for the extra cash. I would get a chance to visit with them as they worked on some of the neighbor's farms. Their English was not always the best. They said the Iowa summer heat was mild to what they were used to in South Texas and Mexico. Eventually, the Green Giant Cannery closed and the migrant workers stopped coming to Vinton. Their camp remained for a number of years, but eventually was razed leaving no evidence of their yearly migration.

Back to our farm, most of the summer field work, consisted of cultivating the crops, baling hay, combining or harvesting oats, and baling straw(animal bedding). The corn and soybean crops took the entire summer to mature and were usually harvested in September & October.

A field of oats or hay did not require any maintenance or cultivation until it was ready to be harvested. The corn and soybeans were a different matter. These were called row crops because they were planted in individual rows. There was a lot of bare ground(about 40 inches) between the rows. This was an ideal spot for weeds to grow until the plants were large enough to shade the ground and the shading stopped many weeds from growing. Until the ground was shaded, you had to eliminate the weeds with a cultivator. Cultivators were mounted or attached directly to tractors. They were a series of sharp, shovel like devices that when lowered into the ground would plow out the weeds, as the tractor moved through the field. They were mounted in such a way that they would not disrupt the corn or soybean plants, only the weeds. Usually, you did a complete cultivation of each field twice. The first time would be when the plants were young and fairly small. You had to drive the tractor very slow because if you went too fast, you could either bury or plow out the newly emerged plants. The second cultivation was timed to be just before the ground was shaded to eliminate as many weeds as possible. You could drive the tractor faster during the second cultivation and this actually did a better job of eliminating weeds. Early cultivators would only handle two rows at a time just like the planters. Four row cultivators quickly followed and made this task go by much quicker.

There was probably no more boring job to do in the field than cultivation. You had to move slowly and concentrate exactly on the row. If you drove too fast or took your eye off the row, you could instantly plow out the plants. It consumed an incredible amount of time, especially with the first cultivators that only took care of two rows. That was one job I would gladly pass off to dad or my brother, but unfortunately I was assigned to the cultivating tasks far more than I wanted. The monotony of the job was only broken at the end of the field, when you extracted the cultivator out of the ground, turned the tractor around, and then headed back down the row. We had many fields that were ½ mile long and they seemed endless when you were cultivating. The only other breaks were when mom or one of the girls would bring out food and drinks for mid morning and mid afternoon lunches. Those lunch breaks did not come soon enough nor ever last long enough to suit me. I certainly had no problem volunteering to do the 5 o'clock cow milking routine.

As stated earlier, both the corn and soybeans were cultivated twice in the summer. Later on, farm chemicals were developed that could be sprayed on the crops to eliminate cultivation. I thought that was an amazing development. You could spray chemicals in a fraction of the time it took to cultivate and those chemicals were smart enough to kill the weeds and not the corn or soybeans. Most of these chemicals however were developed after I had left the farm.

Dad was a real stickler when it came to weeds. He hated them, did not like to see them in his fields, and prided himself as having some of the "cleanest" fields around. His desire to have weed free fields was a curse to me and added many extra hours of work in the summer. It was not at all unusual for dad to know of a particular spot in a corn field that for some reason had lots of weeds that the cultivator did not eliminate. So, if it was a little slow, dad, my brother and I would head out into the corn fields to do a little hand weeding. The corn was usually taller by this time, so you had to walk the corn rows to find the weeds, using a tractor would have smashed the corn plants. We would usually go out in the mornings, when it was cooler. There was a heavy dew on the corn leaves which had you soaking wet in no time. The corn leaves had thin edges that if you were not careful would make small hair line cuts on your face and arms. There were also lots of biting insects as well, which seemed to make a tough job even tougher. Dad had certain weeds he wanted pulled. Most of them pulled with ease, but there seemed to be an unending supply of those pesky things and some were well rooted and did require a lot of strength to pull. I think dad knew this was not a job neither my brother nor I relished and would limit the time to just a few hours and only to mornings when it was cool.

Soybeans offered a unique experience as well. Soybeans were normally planted in a field that had been corn the year before. Corn that did not make it out of the field during the harvest would often times emerge with the freshly planted soybeans, this was called volunteer corn. This made the soybean fields very unsightly and the corn plants would produce ears of corn. When the soybeans were harvested, the corn would mix in with the soybeans. The country elevators that purchased the soybeans would decrease the cost per bushel if it had too much corn mixed with the soybeans. Dad was pretty serious about the volunteer corn as well. He liked seeing his soybean fields free of volunteer corn and he certainly did not want to take a decrease in price if there was corn mixed with the soybeans. Much like weeds in the cornfields, we would set out in the mornings to cut out the volunteer corn. This was not necessarily a "guys only" activity and from time to time, mom and my sisters would join us in "walking the beans". The smart thing to do was hit the bean fields when the soybean plants were small. You could easily step over the rows to get to the corn. You had several options; you could pull the corn, you could hoe it out, or you could just cut it off with a "corn knife", this was more like a small machete than a knife. Normally each person would take four rows of beans and with several persons, you could move through a field of beans in short order. The tough part was if the soybeans got too tall before you eliminated the volunteer corn. If they were waist high or taller, crossing over the rows to get to the corn became major work. The beans were usually wet with a heavy dew and it seemed the taller they were, the more bugs we fought as well. I will say this, when you finished clearing the bean fields of corn, it was rewarding to look across the rows and rows of beans and see nothing but soybeans growing in the warm sun. Dad seemed to be especially proud of his immaculate soy bean field.

Needless to say pulling weeds from the corn fields and corn from the bean fields was not a summer chore I looked forward to. It was a job dad felt had to be done and it was a very rare occasion that I escaped this nasty chore. Another big job in the summer was baling hay.

Baling hay was a lot of work. It required a machine to cut the crop, another machine to concentrate the cut hay into windrows, another machine to pick up the crop and create the bales, the bales were then loaded on a wagon to be hauled to a storage area, and finally the bales had to be stacked away in the storage unit so they could be fed during the winter months. This was a very labor intensive job. Because it required so much physical labor dad cooperated with two of his neighbors Erv and Henry. They each had two sons. Our baling crew consisted of 3 adult men and 6 boys. Generally, right after the first of June, we would bale the hay on Henry's farm, then we would do our hay next, and finally we would bale the hay on Erv's farm. It might require 2-3 days of actual hay baling on each farm. Once the first crop had been baled, it was usually time to bale the 2nd cutting of hay and the process would start all over. We would also help one another bale the oat straw as well. Needless to say, we seemed to spend a lot of summer hours in the hay fields.

Henry would start the hay baling season. His hay crop was mainly alfalfa and it was usually ready to go right after the first of June. As I said before, baling hay was quite labor intensive. The first step was to cut the hay and begin the drying process. A hay mower was attached or pulled by a tractor. The mower had a six foot long blade that contained a series of very sharp cutting blades. These blades were powered by the tractor and moved rapidly back and forth. The plants were cut several inches above the ground and allowed to lie on the plant stubbles. These fresh cut plants had to dry before they could be made into hay bales. This took at least 48 hours to occur. This process could be delayed if the fresh cut hay was rained on. Trying to time when you cut the hay so it would not get rained on was always tricky. Some clever individual invented a machine called a hay conditioner. This machine consisted of two large rubber rollers that smashed or crushed the hay right after it was cut. This reduced the drying time from 48 hours down to 24 hours. It was much easier to time your hay cutting once this machine came on the scene. Another advantage of the hay conditioner was that the quality of the hay was also better.

Once the hay had dried sufficiently it was time to make it into bales. Before that however, those long flat rows of cut hay had to be placed in windrows by a machine called a hay rake. The hay rake had a series of wire like teeth that picked the hay off the ground and stacked it in these long flowing windrows. When the windrowing process was complete, the hay field looked like a giant continuous maze stretched over the field.

Now the hay was ready for baling. The actual baling process usually started after the noon meal. The dew had to be off the windrows and the hay sufficiently dry. The hay baler was actually quite an interesting piece of farm equipment. It was pulled by and powered by a tractor. In the front of the baler were a series of wire like teeth that picked the hay off the ground and fed it into the baling chamber. Once in the chamber a large plunger would smash and compress the hay into bales, much like our garbage trucks and trash compactors. To keep the bales together, the baler would wrap two sets of twine around each bale and tie the twine into knots so the bales would not break apart. The newly formed bales would then be forced down a shoot or bale chamber and onto a wagon that was being pulled behind the baler. On the wagon, the bales were extracted by a strong body and then the bales were stacked on the wagon. Stacking the hay was like using giant building blocks. One bale's length equaled the width of two bales. So, the bales were placed in stacks alternating them back and forth until there were four layers high each stack containing 16 bales. The wagons were designed to hold about 60-64 bales. When the wagon was full, it was disconnected from the baler, an empty wagon was hooked up and the process would start all over again. The full load of hay was then taken to the farmstead where it was unloaded into a barn, storage shed, or a special structure designed for holding hay called a hay barracks.

With three families baling hay together, we developed a very finely tuned hay making operation. In the field, one person would drive the tractor that pulled the hay baler and wagon. Two people would be on the hay rack. One would pull the bales out of the baler and throw them to the back of the wagon where the other person would stack them. After the wagon was full, we would rotate so that you would not do the same thing all the time, one would drive, one would stack bales, and one would extract the bales. Another person would deliver the empty wagon to the baling crew and deliver the full load of hay to the storage area. At the storage area, one person would unload the hay and two others would stack it away in the hay mow, hay barracks, etc. Usually the hay was thrown off the wagon into an elevator which then transported the hay into the storage facility. I usually was on the hay baling crew or drove the wagons back and forth to and from the fields. I actually did not mind the hay baling other than the heat and humidity was stifling. The hay bales weighed from 50-60 pounds and required some effort to hoist them over your head and stack them on the wagon. However, you were always working with someone and the conversations were usually fun. Also, after you stacked the wagon, it was your turn to drive the tractor pulling the baler, so you got to rest up before your next rotation. My body became very lean and mean. I wasn't pumping iron, but I was pumping a lot of hay and burning up tons of calories in the hot Iowa sun. On a good day, we could easily bale over a 1000 bales of hay and make quick work of a big hay field. I never envied the people who had to store the hay away, which were usually the dads. If the hay was going in a barn, it was usually very hot inside the barns with little or no air circulating. Although it was hot in the fields, it was much hotter inside those barns. I guess the fathers wanted to make sure the hay was properly stored and that is why the kids were rarely asked to help with the storing.

Afternoon lunch breaks were always a must. These occurred about 3 PM and provided by the women on whosever farm we were working. Lunches were usually cold meat sandwiches, chips, lots of fresh lemonade, and cookies or cake. Those lunches really hit the spot and charged up the batteries for the rest of the afternoon. Lunch time was also entertainment time especially when we were working on Henry's farm. His wife Audrey would always deliver the lunches to the baling crew in the field. You knew lunch was coming because of the cloud of dust that flowed from Audrey's car as she sped out to the fields. There were no real roads through the farm fields, only dirt paths. She would really have her pedal to the metal and it's hard to believe she did not cause major damage to her car as she bounced along. She would come roaring up to the baler, slam on the breaks and would often emerge from the car before it had totally stopped. Audrey was quite a talker and her mouth was always going a mile a minute. She would grab the food and drinks out of the back seat and bring them to us. She would usually have to rebuild the sandwiches since the trip out pretty much wreaked havoc with them. She would be talking as fast as she could, asking many questions, but rarely waiting for the answer before moving onto the next question. We would usually be doubled over with laughter listening to her stories and at times I think we were laughing more because of her than with her. Once lunch was done, she would gather up the remains of lunch, throw it in the car and blaze away in a cloud of dust. After some good food and drink, a few laughs, and some rest, it was back to making hay. Most of the time we would stop baling around 6 PM. We all had chores to do and both dad and Henry had cows to milk. Usually one person would break away a little early to start the milking process.

Once all the hay was baled at Henry's farm, we would go to our farm where the process was repeated, and then on to Erv's farm after we were done. It was not a continual process day after day. You were always at the mercy of the weather and sometimes you had to wait and let the hay crop mature before you could cut it. Baling hay and making straw certainly did occupy many summer hours.

Another event that consumed some time was combining the oats. As the years rolled on, this required less and less time since the number of acres planted to this crop declined. The oat crop required little or no attention until it needed to be harvested. It grew quickly and usually by early July the pale green stalks and heads of grain were a golden yellow color. Dad would usually cut the oats much like hay and place it in windrows to be picked up by the combine. Others would simply pull their combines through the fields behind their tractors cutting and thrashing the grain in one step. Combines in the fifties were usually small and had to be pulled by a tractor, there were very few self-contained or what were called self-propelled combines. The capacity of these combines was small and in order for them to work; they had to be pulled slowly through the fields. They would consume the oat plants, head and stalks, and separate the grain from the stalks or stems. The grain would be placed in a large bin on the combine and the stalks would be discharged out of the back of the combine onto the ground. When the combine bin was full, it would be dumped into a grain wagon. When that wagon was full, it would be taken to the farmstead, unloaded into an elevator, and then conveyed to a storage bin, usually inside the granary/corn crib. Although there was not a lot of physical labor involved in harvesting oats, it was a dirty, itchy job. As the oats were processed, lots of chaff, dust, and other debris were released into the air. This debris would quickly cling to a sweaty body and set up a lot of irritation, especially in those body crevices in the arm pits. Nothing felt better than hopping in the shower at the end of the day and getting rid of that itchy chaff.

Once the oats had been harvested, the stems or straw remained in the fields. This made excellent bedding material for the livestock in the winter time. The straw was made into bales much like the hay was. It was made into windrows by the hay rake and then a baler came along and made it into bales. It was stored in the barns as well and used in the winter for livestock bedding. Many farmers also placed straw bales around the foundations of their house in the winter as well. It was very good insulation against the strong winter cold and wind.

I quickly learned there was always something to do on the farm especially in the summer when you could work outside almost every day. With so many buildings on the farmstead, small repairs were always in order and from time to time bigger projects like shingling a roof had to be done. Barnyard fences were usually made out of wood and they needed repair or painting. The farm equipment needed constant maintenance and repair. The yards around the buildings needed to be mowed and weeds had to be pulled or cut. Mom was always looking for an extra hand to help in the garden or help prepare the vegetables for freezing or canning.

Mom's garden became almost a full time job in and of itself. It was huge and it was so big that some years, there were two or three plots around the farmstead. She would have dad till the garden plots and then she would start working the soil for her vegetables. She would plant, radishes, carrots, peas, beans, cucumbers, squash, pumpkins, potatoes and a variety of ornamental gourds. She would get starter plants such as cabbage and tomato from a local nursery and plant them at the appropriate time. Asparagus and strawberries were perennials and would emerge on their own. She would plant each vegetable in long straight rows. Whenever she had a spare moment, she would be out there wedding and hoeing. Like dad, she took a great deal of pride in having a weed free garden. Each vegetable would mature at a certain time. Everything had to be hand picked. Mom would then wash them and depending on the vegetable or fruit, she would can them or freeze them. When certain vegetables were mature, such as green beans, it could be an all day project to pick them, clean them, cut them into small pieces and then prepare them for canning or freezing. Mom had this big old pressure cooker that she would load up with several jars of vegetables. This was then heated on the stove to complete the canning process. Although it never happened at our house, you would hear of pressure cookers exploding and causing major injury to humans and houses. On these big canning days, mom would enlist the help of anyone with a pair of hands. Once the vegetables were canned and the jars cooled, they would be carried down to the basement and stored on the shelves in the fruit cellar.

Mom did not plant any sweet corn in her garden. Dad would usually plant several rows of sweet corn in one of the fields of corn near the house. When it was ready, we would usually head out right after breakfast and pick several dozen ears of corn. We would remove all the husks and silk in the field and bring the freshly husked ears back to the house. Mom would then wash it, cut it off the cob, cook it, and then freeze it. We would always save a few ears to boil on the stove for fresh corn on the cob. It was always so good, but it seemed after many days of fresh corn on the cob, even that got a little old. The local raccoon population usually discovered our sweet corn patch as well. It was so aggravating, because they would pull ear after ear down off the stalk and then only eat a portion of the corn, leaving the rest exposed and worthless.

Mom always grew a lot of potatoes as well. These had to be hand dug, cleaned, and then stored away down in the fruit cellar to be eaten in the winter time. Mom did not can any potatoes. Mom would convert fresh cabbage into tangy sauerkraut. She would take fresh cucumbers and make a variety of pickles including; dills, bread and butters, and sweet pickles.

Mom would also can certain fruits that we could not raise on the farm such as peaches and Bing cherries. She would drive into town and purchase crates or bushels of fresh fruit. She would bring them home and they too were cleaned, canned, and stored away in the fruit cellar. By the end of the summer, the fruit cellar was full of potatoes, pumpkins, gourds, beans, sauerkraut, beets, carrots, pickles, cherries, and peaches. These would be brought up during the winter. Although they were not quite as good as fresh picked, mom's home canned creations were very good.

One job I detested about as much as I detested corn and bean walking was repairing fences. The fences around the farmstead were wood and they were simple to fix. However, we had miles of fences that separated individual fields and our land from the neighbors. These fences consisted of wooden fence posts, galvanized woven wire mesh, and strands of barb wire. It seemed there were certain fences that were always being damaged either by flooding streams or livestock that wanted to test the limits of the fence. Dad always wanted to repair these fences rather than tear them out and replace them. He was a great tinkerer when it came to fences. We would sometimes spend hours putzing around with those fences and when we finished I was not sure we had really improved on the situation. It seemed like an exercise in futility. To me, that was a job better left to dad alone because he knew how much I hated doing it.

Summer started winding down in mid August. The hay
and straw had been baled, the crops cultivated, and the oats
harvested. Harvesting the corn and soy beans could not begin until
September. The county fair was the first week in August and that
was a really big deal to a farm kid. I will cover that in a chapter
devoted to The Fair. This was the time for lots of odd jobs to be
done and maybe reduce the work pace a little bit. Rural schools
started in late August so dad tried to squeeze all he could from his
cheap labor before school started once again.

Fall

The main focus of fall was to get the corn and soybeans
harvested and safely stored away before winter arrived. It was
also a time to get the farmstead ready for winter. It was one of my
favorite seasons. It started getting a little cooler, but not real cold.
The leaves on the hardwood trees would turn to brilliant shades
of gold, orange, and red. For some reason harvesting the fall crops
was more fun than work. It was also football season and that was a
major happening in small rural towns every Friday night. Fall was
also hunting season, which many farm kids and dads loved to do.

Just as summer would start the 1st of June, fall would start the
1st of September rather than the 21st. The first major event on the
fall agenda was harvesting the soybeans. The soybean plants would
turn brown in late August or early September. Their leaves would
fall off leaving the bean stalk exposing the shriveled up bean pods
that would have 2-3 soybeans per pod. The soybeans could not
be combined until they had adequately dried in the fields. If the
beans were stored with too much moisture in them, they could get
moldy and then be worthless. The combine that harvested the oats
was modified slightly for the soybean harvest. The early combines
were pulled through the fields with tractors. The beans were cut
off by the combine and separated from the stems and delivered to
the bin on the combine. Periodically the bin was emptied into a
wagon, which when full was taken to the farmstead, and the beans
stored in the granary just like oats. Later on, combines became self

contained or self propelled. They also became larger and larger and today are literally behemoths that can combine many acres of soybeans in a single day. Dad bought his first self propelled combine after I graduated from high school and was in college. I enjoyed coming home from college on weekends and running that huge machine. We normally stored the soybeans for sometime. We did not use them for animal food, but would sell them to the local grain elevator when the price improved. The soybean harvest did not usually take too long, because initially it was a small crop. Like many outdoor activities the harvest was mainly dependant on the weather.

Harvesting the corn crop was always the main activity on the farm. It was the largest crop in terms of acres planted and it was also the main source of food for the farm animals. The corn harvest usually started in mid to late September. Like soybeans, the corn had to dry in the fields before it could be stored in the granaries. For a long time, the corn was picked and stored as whole ears of corn. At one time, men had to walk down the rows of corn, hand pick each ear, and throw it in a wagon pulled by horses. Mechanical corn pickers virtually revolutionized how the corn was harvested. Corn pickers were large machines mounted directly on a tractor or some were pulled by a tractor like a hay baler. These were loud, banging, dangerous machines. They would strip the ears off two rows of corn with large metal rollers and then convey the ears to a wagon pulled behind the corn picker. Sometimes stalks would jam up in the rollers. Farmers that got in a hurry to free the clogged stalks would try to do this when the picker was running. Unfortunately some lost a hand to their carelessness and some even were killed. It was not unusual at all to see a farmer with a "metal hook" on one arm. The usual answer for the "hook" was lost it in a corn picker accident.

Dad and Erv shared a corn picker as long as I could remember. They purchased the machine together and then would help one another harvest the corn crop. The kids were in school and could only help on the weekends. Usually Erv would run the picker on dad's farm and dad would run the picker on Erv's farm. The one who was not running the corn picker would haul the full loads of corn into the corn crib and unload it and then return with the empty wagon. This was much easier than having to stop every time there was a full load of corn and haul it in yourself, unload it, go back to the field and then pick another load of corn. I enjoyed the corn harvest season. The work was not hard or dirty and the weather was cool, but not cold. I would try and help out after school or on weekends. My job was usually hauling the full loads of corn in from the field and then unloading them. The corn was dumped into the elevator, which then conveyed the corn into the corn crib. It was always a challenge to get the corn unloaded and back to the field with the empty wagon before the next wagon was full. Most years the corn harvest was done by the end of October. However, if the weather did not cooperate, you might still be picking corn well into November. I remember one particularly bad fall when we had a lot of rain and some very early snows and we did not finish the corn harvest until Thanksgiving.

Once the corn harvest was done, preparations for winter usually started. Sometimes we did some fall plowing, trying to get a jump on the spring planting season. There was usually a certain amount of "winterizing" that took place as well. Sheds and barns were made less drafty. All of the watering devices for the livestock had to have some type of heating device to keep the water from freezing. Our old house was pretty well insulated and dad had installed some combination windows, so we did not have to replace the summer screens with winter storm windows. When winter arrived was always a little unpredictable. Cold and snow could come as early as October or it might not arrive until December. We did not always have a white Christmas. Once the corn was harvested, the pace slowed quite a bit and jobs were done as long as weather permitted.

One activity I enjoyed a lot was hunting. This was a sport that lots of people in our rural area enjoyed as well. Hunting pheasants was the most popular hunting sport. Hunting season opened the first weekend in November. Most all of the leaves were off the trees, the corn fields had been picked, and the hay

and pasture grounds had been turned brown with the fall freezing
temperatures. Pheasant hunting was somewhat of a social sport.
Two or three fathers and their sons would get together and walk
the fields in search of the ring-necked pheasants. We did not
have a hunting dog that could sniff out where the pheasants were
hiding. We would just walk up and down the fields with 20-30
feet between each person. We would hope our noisy feet and our
conversation would flush the pheasants from their hiding spots. It
was amazing how these birds, about the size of a chicken, could
hide so well. In some cases you would almost have to step on
them to flush them into flight. It seems pheasants would both
freeze and not fly or they would hear you coming and fly out
many yards ahead, well out of range of our shotguns. When the
rooster pheasant would take to flight, he always did so with a loud
cackling sound, which if he was close would scare the daylights
out of you. I am sure he was trying to startle you so much your aim
would be errant and he could continue on his merry way. When
I first started hunting it was very frustrating. Being young and
inexperienced, I was often late in bringing my gun to my shoulder
and the older more experienced hunters would have already
dropped the bird by the time I was ready to shoot. Eventually, I
did get my first pheasant in the game bag and as time went on,
I too became one of the more experienced hunters. Dad and the
other fathers eventually stayed at home and the "youngsters" did
the hunting. It was great fun getting together with high school
buddies on the weekend for socializing and hunting. We would be
disappointed if we didn't bring some birds home, but we enjoyed
being out in the crisp fall air, the drama of stalking the birds, and
the good times we had in conversation. If the weather cooperated,
pheasant hunting became a weekend ritual until the season closed,
usually the end of December.

As I said earlier, I enjoyed the fall season a great deal.
Unfortunately, Iowa winters followed those pleasant fall days. Each
day that passed had fewer and fewer daylight hours so that by early
December it was dark by 5 PM.

Winter

Once again, the start of winter was more determined by the activities and the weather than a date on the calendar. Winters in Iowa would vary a lot from year to year, much as they still do now. Temperatures could be bitterly cold, negative 15-20 degrees below zero with strong winds, 20-30 mph, driving wind chill temperatures to the negative 50-60 degrees below zero. Snow fall amounts could also vary a lot. Some years snowfall would only be several inches. Other years you could have many inches of snow which when piled up by the winds could be several feet deep. Blizzards would come through from time to time. These storms were characterized with heavy snowfall and driving winds. Blizzards would drift the snow so badly that you could not drive down many roads. It would not be unusual to be snow bound for a few days before the county snow plow could come down our rural road and plow our road free of snow. The kids loved snow storms because it usually meant no school for a day or two. Mom was maybe not as enthusiastic, but I think she enjoyed the opportunity of having us all inside and did her best to entertain us.

The cold and snow was tough on the animals. Barns were not heated and often times were drafty. The pigs would tend to pile up when they slept to conserve body heat. The cows tended to stay in their barns, but would wander out into the yards for a little exercise and to hit the feed and watering troughs. Surprisingly, there was little frost bite in the animals and little or no death loss due to hypothermia. Cattle seemed to be amazingly tough. They could be out in the cold with their backs covered with snow and seem perfectly content to be chewing on a clump of hay.

Our activities outside around the farmstead were pretty limited, especially when it was bitterly cold. Dad always kept the water troughs from freezing. He would venture out several times a day to make sure the little burners under the water troughs were burning. These were little fuel oil burners that had to be filled frequently so they would not run out of fuel. There were probably a half dozen or so watering troughs scattered around the farm which kept him very busy some days. All of our animals needed to be fed as well. The grains and hay we had harvested in the summer and fall now had to be taken out of storage and delivered to the animals. The pigs ate out of big round metal feeders and went through feed much faster to keep up their body heat. Cattle consumed huge quantities of hay and grain as well.

Since I was in school, I just did a few chores in the morning and night. There was not much else that could be done. However, when the weekend came, there were other jobs to be done. This was a good time to prepare the animal feed for the week ahead. Most of our livestock feed was not just simple grains. Their feed was usually a combination of corn and supplements that had to be ground and mixed together. Cattle feed was usually whole ears of corn that were ground up cobs and all and then mixed with a supplement. Grinding feed was labor intensive. You had to get the feed grinder up to the corn crib and then shovel the ears of corn into a hopper. Once the feed was ground, it was put in a wagon and hauled to the appropriate barn for feeding. Hogs could not handle the corn cobs, so their feed was shelled corn that was ground and mixed with supplements. We had a special wagon where the ground feed was dumped. It had a series of augers that could move the prepared feed directly to a hog feeder or storage bin in the barns. This was quite a labor savings device since prior to its invention the ground feed would have to be hand shoveled off the wagon. Unfortunately it did not matter what the weather was like, the animals had to eat and the feed had to be made. I can remember grinding feed on the weekends when it was bitterly cold and wondering if I was going to survive.

Our dairy cows still needed to be milked twice a day, no matter how cold the weather. It took all I could do some mornings to roll out of bed and get ready, knowing just how cold it was outside. I could often times hear the wind howling around our house. Out of all the barns, the dairy barn seemed to be the warmest. Those old cows threw off a lot of body heat but it was still a very cold job. The barn cats would usually gather in the area where the dairy cows stayed at night. They would huddle near the cows and the braver ones would actually rest on the cows' backs. I was surprised the cows would let them perch there. The cats certainly benefited more from this sleeping arrangement than the cows. My feet always seemed to get cold first and there were times when I did not think they would ever thaw out. On those bitterly cold days, we seemed to move a little faster as we were anxious to get back to the house where it was nice and toasty and mom would have a large hot meal waiting for us.

Entertaining ourselves in the winter was limited to very few outdoor activities. Living in Iowa, there were no large mountains to ski on, very few lakes to do ice fishing, and snow mobiles were not even invented. Our small creeks would freeze over and there would be a few stretches where the creeks widened out where you could ice skate. This was not always predictable as well and often times the ice was rough and not very conducive for skating. Often times after a snow and before the county snow plow cleared our gravel road we could sled down the country roads. Our farmstead sat on top of a small rolling hill. The road that led past the house had a nice gentle pitch in either direction from the house. When conditions were just right, you could have a nice ¼ mile ride down the hill on your sled. You always had to be a little careful, however, as you shared your sledding space with the local cars and trucks.

Not too far from our home, the gently rolling country side turned into some rather larger hills with a fairly good pitch to them. I believe we called it Thompson's hill. This was a gathering spot for many of the neighborhood kids. Sometimes as many as 20-30 children would congregate to test their sledding skills. It was a great area as it was just a large hill with an occasional tree or two; some nice little dips down the side, and lots of room for lots of sleds and toboggans. When conditions were just right, you could have some awesome rides down that hill. There was only one hazard on the course. At the bottom of the hill there was a fairly long stretch of pasture, but at the end was a small creek at the bottom of a deep ravine. If you had a great ride, you could make it to the ravine. The trick was to bale off your sled or toboggan before you got to the ravine. It was sure disaster if you did not. It was great fun to pile 4 or 5 bodies on a toboggan and go sailing down the hill side. The ride could get a little rough and sometimes a body would fly off the toboggan. If you were the unlucky one to fall off, you hoped somebody on a sled was not going to run over you as they went whisking by. With all the kids, sleds, and toboggans, you would have thought there would have been lots of accidents, but there were not many. Some cuts, scrapes, and bruises, but I don't remember anyone getting broken bones. It did not take long before the cold snow soaked through your clothes and you began to feel the winter cold. Sometimes there would be a roaring bon fire to warm up around, or you would retreat to the car or pick up to do the same. If it was really cold, 20-30 minutes of sledding and you were ready to pack it in and head home.

Most of our snow storms in Iowa amounted to only a few inches of snow. However, the occasional blizzard would come through and leave many inches of snow. These heavy snows were accompanied by driving winds that piled the snow many feet high. Those huge banks of snow were ideal for carving out snow caves and tunnels. The heavy wet snows were also ideal for making snowballs and snowmen. My brother and I would always try to make the biggest snowmen around. We would roll the snow into huge balls and stack them up as high as we could. Our snowmen were often eight feet tall or higher. There were always lots of snowball fights with neighborhood kids or at school during recess. They always sounded like a lot of fun until you got hit in the face with of those ice cold missiles and after a short period of time the snowballs had soaked your mittens and your fingers were frozen stiff. The snow was always neat at first, but when it soaked through to your skin, it was not that much fun.

Farm Cooking

The meals my mom prepared when we were on the farm were awesome. If you asked me when I was 12 years old, I would have said my mom was a good cook. However, as you get older and move away from home and have to cook for yourself or eat dorm food, you realize how good that "on the farm home cook'n" was. When I recall the meals my mom made, it's hard to imagine she had time to do anything else but cook. Remember this was the time before microwaves and frozen dinners. Most meals were prepared from scratch and much of the food we ate on the farm was raised there as well. We raised our own meat, poultry, milk, eggs, and vegetables. Mom's grocery shopping was buying other raw ingredients such as flour and sugar and canning supplies. Also, remember that we ate three large meals every day, breakfast, dinner, and supper. When we were busy with field work, there were also mid morning and mid afternoon lunch breaks.

Breakfast is emphasized today as an important meal, it certainly was very important on the farm. As I said earlier, we would milk the cows and do a few morning chores before having breakfast. Getting up early and milking those cows got your body awake and got your appetite going. I always liked breakfast, but it was very special coming in from the winter's cold to a good hot meal. Dad liked his coffee and that was usually the first thing you smelled as we came in the back door. Mixed with the coffee aroma would be the smell of bacon, sausage, or ham frying in the skillet.

One of mom's pride and joys was a large electric skillet where she would fry the eggs, in melted butter of course. Several times a week, the smell of cinnamon would also be in the air. Mom would make fresh cinnamon rolls from scratch and they were a very special treat for breakfast. If we did not have cinnamon rolls, there was always lots of toast. Our meal of eggs, meat, and bread, would be topped off with a big bowl of cereal. In the summer, that would be cold cereal and in the winter it would be hot cereal such as oatmeal or "cream of wheat". After breakfast, it was get ready for school, or back outside to do more farm work when school was out.

During times of heavy field work, spring, summer, and fall, mom would prepare a light lunch around 10:00 am. This was usually cold meat sandwiches, chips, and something to drink such as home made lemonade or cool aid. She was not real fond of soda pop, so that was rarely on the menu. If we were working in the fields away from the farmstead, mom would often times bring the lunch to us in the field. This saved us a lot of time and got the field work done faster.

During the summer months, the noon meal or dinner as we called it was a big meal. I think the reason we called it dinner instead of lunch was because the meal was so big. Dad was not real big on casseroles, so our meals were meat, potatoes, vegetables, and desserts. Dad always tried to stick to the same schedule every day and I think mom appreciated that. Breakfast was at 6:30 AM, dinner was at noon, and supper was at 6:00 PM. The smells were always good as we came in the back door. Mom would always boil potatoes for dinner and make home made gravy from the meat she was cooking. Our meat was steak of some kind, pork chops, or fried chicken. There was only one way mom cooked meat, very well done. The meat was usually fried and often breaded with flour. I was probably a senior in high school before I realized there were other ways to cook a steak besides well done. Our vegetables were usually fresh from the garden in the summer or in the winter time, we ate vegetables that mom had canned in the summer. Unless you have eaten vegetables fresh from the garden, you just can not describe their taste. Home grown vegetables are picked when they are ripe and usually eaten the day they are picked. Again, you can not describe the taste, it has to be experienced. Dinner also came with lots of bread or home made rolls. Dessert was never an option it was always a part of the meal. Home made pies and cakes were the usual fare. Fresh fruits such as strawberries, peaches, and apples were also part of the dessert menu. I can remember my grandpa Rinderknecht putting a big slice of shortcake in the bottom of a bowl, piling that high with strawberries, and then pouring lots of cream over the whole thing. Funny grandpa Rinderknecht never had high cholesterol, high blood pressure, or heart disease. Mom's desserts were the best; especially her made from scratch sour cream chocolate cake and her apple pie. She won a number of prizes at the county fair for her apple pies. At that time, I just thought everybody ate like we did. Dessert was often two pieces of pie or a piece of pie and a piece of cake. It would almost be insulting if you only had one serving of dessert. What was even more remarkable was the fact that when we had neighbors over helping with haying, mom would feed them as well. This was another six people to feed along with her family of seven. It never seemed to be that big a deal to her. The meal was always ready at noon, it was always hot, and it was always delicious.

After the noon meal, dad had to have his little nap. Usually he was out by 12:30, but like clock work, he was awake at 1 PM and out of the house we would go for the afternoon work.

Another lunch break would come around 2:30 PM. This was pretty much an instant replay of the morning lunch. Field work would wrap up late in the afternoon, the chores would get done and then back to the house for supper. Supper was really not a lot different than dinner. Potatoes, meats, vegetables and desserts were the fare. The meats and veggies would be different at each meal and almost always they were raised on our farm. All of the vegetables we raised on the farm were excellent. Fresh peas, green beans, tomatoes, and sweet corn were my favorites. We did not have a lot of luck growing melons, but we had some farm families that seemed to specialize in growing cantaloupe and watermelons.

Desserts were also a big part of supper. Mom would often times have ice cream to go along with the pies and cakes.

After supper, we would retire in front of the TV for the night's entertainment. Some times in the summer, we would return to the fields and work until it got dark. You would have thought that with all the food we consumed during the day, we would have needed no more before bed time. That was not the case as Dad would usually need a little snack before turning in. Popcorn popped in the skillet with lots of melted butter was one of his favorites. Occasionally mom would make some caramel corn as well. If there was no popcorn, there were candy bars, cookies, or something sweet as a bed time treat.

I can't imagine how many calories we must have consumed in a day back then. We just worked so hard and so long that we burnt them up every day. Believe me, in those days no one in our family was overweight.

As I said earlier, I had little or no appreciation of how hard mom worked to prepare all that food. I think I first realized how special her efforts were, when I left for college and started eating some of that delicious dorm food. Coming home for weekends, quarter breaks, and holidays became even more special as I looked forward to that down on the farm home cook'n. She never considered some of the foods she prepared to be all that special, but there were certain things she made that can not be duplicated. Her homemade egg noodles were fantastic. Her homemade sauerkraut was particularly tangy. She made several varieties of pickles in the summer with her dill pickles being the best. I am not sure if she ever made a bad dessert but the ones I remember the most were, apple pies, cherry pies, pecan pies, my brothers' favorite, chocolate cakes, and other concoctions made with rice, whipped cream, and tapioca. I can get very hungry just thinking about all those foods, most were prepared from scratch with fresh ingredients, and hours and hours of hard work and love. Dad was never real big on handing out compliments, but he did rave about mom's apple pie.

Gene's confrimation with Dad & Jolene

Gene's Church Confirmation Class

Trintiy Lutheran Church - Gene's home church

The Church

Our family belonged to a small Missouri Synod Lutheran Church in the town of Vinton. It was one of several churches in that small town. It would have been very unusual in that time not to be involved in a church. I think there were two different Lutheran churches in our town of 5,000 people. There was a Catholic church and many other Christian churches as well.

A great deal of the social activities revolved around the church at that time. Everyone went to their church on Sunday morning. There was Sunday school of course. Our church also had Saturday school every Saturday morning during the school year for those students going through confirmation. There were activities for the youngsters and for the adults as well. It was certainly an outlet for social gatherings and entertainment. My parents would gather at the church with other couples on Sunday nights to play cards. That group was called the Fireside Club. The kids would usually take in a movie at the local theatre while the adults played cards.

Many of the kids in our church were neighbors as well. They were also in the same schools so we became a fairly close knit group. As I recall, we did not do a lot of things back then. We would attend some summer camps, have some softball games in the summer, and have some sledding parties in the winter. Our youth gatherings were held monthly and we would have bible study at church and maybe play some games as well. Although it gave you something to do, it was not the most exciting of times.

Sunday school seemed to have its ups and downs. It seemed like it could be a lot of fun or pretty boring depending on your teacher. The Sunday school teachers were usually the moms of the church. Some of them were very strict and tough disciplinarians which did not make for much fun. Others tried to make bible study interesting and applicable to events of the day. We did not do too much outside of the Sunday morning class time. Once in a while, we would sing a little song in church. The big event for the Sunday school kids was the annual Christmas program. Our Christmas program was always held on Christmas Eve. The program would vary a little bit from year to year. Some years we would do a Christmas pageant, some years we would just sing a lot of Christmas songs. We would always recite bible verses relating to the Christmas story during the program. This was always a big deal. Each child was given a bible verse to memorize several weeks before the program. The youngest children were given very short verses and the older ones had longer verses. Mom would grill us pretty hard to make sure we could say our verses without mistakes. On Christmas Eve, everyone was so excited and it was hard to concentrate on reciting your bible verse. I usually said my verse without too much trouble. However, some of those little kids had quite a time. They would stumble and stammer through their verses and usually needed a little prodding from one of the Sunday school teachers. It was an event everyone looked forward to and everyone seemed to enjoy, especially the parents. The best part of the night was the bag of candy you received after you left church. It was just a plain brown bag, but there were lots of goodies in it; peanuts, candy bars, candy canes, tootsie rolls, and the like. It was a nice little stash to have in your bedroom and dip into when you needed a little treat. It was the tradition in our family to go home after church and open our Christmas presents on Christmas Eve, Santa Claus always dropped by and left the presents while we were in church. More on this later.

Easter was also a very big church event. Lent was usually ushered in with an Ash Wednesday service and then every Wednesday after that, Lenten services were held until Easter.

I always liked the Easter season as well. I think the reason I enjoyed it so much, was Easter usually signaled the end of the winter season and warmer weather was just around the corner. Depending on what Sunday Easter was celebrated, it also signaled the beginning of planting season, or we were well into the spring planting season. Somehow, that Easter bunny always managed to find our house and leave some colored eggs, jelly beans, and lots of chocolate covered goodies. I loved those chocolate covered marshmallow Easter bunnies. Church services on Easter were always special. The ladies would always wear their finest new spring wardrobe and back then, they usually had a new Easter bonnet as well. I don't recall any Easter parades however, where the ladies could strut their stuff down Main Street. It was amazing how some of those farm ladies could clean up and look down right pretty if they worked at it.

Sometime in the summer, the church ladies would usually have a big ice cream social. The men would gather the ice cream makers and gather at the church to make home made ice cream. It was a lot of work, as most of the ice cream churns had to be "hand cranked". Each would bring their favorite recipe for ice cream, each hoping to out do the other for taste and uniqueness. The ladies would bring their finest, pies, cakes, and pastries. Before all that delicious food was consumed, the men would play a little softball or pitch some horse shoes. The ladies would sit around and visit or play cards. Some would bring their crafts such as crochet and work on that while they visited. When the ice cream was done, it was time to chow down on all those delicious desserts. It was so hard to decide what to eat, but one thing was for sure, I always had some of mom's apple pie, because it was the best, bar none. Some fresh home made vanilla ice cream on top of that piece of pie was indescribable.

Thanksgiving also was also celebrated in the church. Being a rural community, there was much to celebrate after the crops had been harvested and another season of hard labor was rewarded with a bountiful crop. It signaled the completion of the growing season and back then, signaled the beginning of the Christmas season.

It was almost a sin to begin advertising Christmas merchandise before Thanksgiving. Our small church and small town would do their best to decorate for the coming Christmas holiday. It was a special time of preparation between Thanksgiving and Christmas.

Verna & Gene going fishing 1953

Gene & Dad touring Morman Feed Plant

The Local Hangouts & Diversions

Growing up in rural Iowa in the 50's was challenging from the stand point of entertainment and things to do. Like every generation of young people, there was just nothing to do for kids. There were not many places to go to or things to do. However, I would like to touch on a few of the places I would go to meet up with friends and classmates. These "hangouts" were places where you would go once you could drive a car. Prior to having a car, you pretty much went with your parents or found things to do on the farm itself.

There was a little Café/diner right on main street in "downtown" Vinton, called Cronk's café. Like many diners back then, there were a handful of booths and a few tables and chairs. It was certainly not a fancy place, the walls were faded, the floor tiles were worn, and a few pictures hung on the walls. A juke box was in one corner and at each booth was a small box that accepted coins to play the juke box. There was just a greasy kind of feel when you walked in the front door. However, the smells were fantastic and a friendly little waitress always greeted you with a smile and a "howdy". You could sit any where there was an empty chair or booth. The menus were just a single sheet of paper covered with plastic with a mustard or ketchup stain on them. The fare at that time was mainly sandwiches, fries, and sodas. There were "regular" meals and blue plate specials as well. Us kids, however, would usually do the burgers, fries, and coke routine. I don't remember the prices, but I am sure all three items together were less than a buck. Lots of good conversations developed over those burgers and fries while the latest rock and roll songs blared from the juke box. There was never any pressure to make you move on, just as long as no one got out of hand. There was an occasional ketchup or mustard fight, but for the most part we were good, probably just a little loud and boisterous.

Not too far from Cronk's café was Leach's Ice Cream parlor. This was also a very small place and was designed more for grabbing something and taking it with you. It certainly had more of a following in the summer than during the winter months. They were especially famous for their homemade, hand squeezed, lemonade. I can remember going there after late summer football practice and guzzling down several of those large lemonades, truly refreshing! I believe they were one of the few places that had air conditioning as well. Because it was a little smaller place, you did not do a lot of "hanging out" there, but you would often make your purchase and go outside and relax on the steps while you consumed your ice cream, lemonade, etc.

Right across the street from Cronk's Café was the Palace Movie Theater. It was a small movie theatre, but certainly a popular spot to take your favorite gal or to see a movie with a group of friends. Being a small theatre in a small town, there were not a lot of first run movies showing. However, the big hits did eventually make it to the Palace. I remember seeing Alfred Hitchcock's thriller, Psycho; lots of westerns, and some of Elvis Presley's early flicks. Even that "racy" movie <u>A Summer Place</u> made it to town and had the "locals" talking for some time. The popcorn was certainly the best and I think only 5 cents for a bag and maybe ten cents for a coke. The Palace struggled to stay open and did close from time to time. I believe to this day movies are still shown there.

During the summer months, two "drive-in" hamburger stands opened for the season, A & W Root Beer and the "Dog'n Suds. These were your typical drive-ins where you pulled up with your car and a cute little waitress would come to your car and take your order. These drive-ins were pre-fast food restaurants so each order was prepared individually. Both drive-ins had great burgers, fries, and milk shakes. One was located on the south side of town, the other on the northwest side about two miles apart. Which one you stopped at was determined by how crowded they were or who had the better looking waitresses that night. It was pretty much standard procedure to give the waitress a hard time or see if somehow you could drive off with one of those large glass root beer steins. Yes, all the drinks were served in "frosty" glass steins, not paper or Styrofoam. It was difficult to take one of those mugs, however, the owners and the waitresses had a system and knew exactly if their tray was short a mug. These two drive-ins were great places to meet your friends. There was lots of "back and forth" between the parked cars. I am sure the people there with their families did not appreciate the loud teenagers and the car "honking" that went on. The Dog'n Suds drive-in was just a ¼ mile from the county fairgrounds. So, in early August when the fairgrounds were in action, there was lots of traffic at this spot. Like many restaurants, they employed high school students. My younger sisters took their turn as waitresses and kitchen help. Before they could drive, it was my job to pick them up after the night shift. I would usually show up a little early to see if there was any left over food and try and embarrass my sisters a little. They did not seem to appreciate my lame attempts of humor.

In a small rural town, there were no teen clubs, YMCA, or indoor arcades. We did have a small bowling alley, which I rarely went to and we also had an indoor roller rink. Although, I enjoyed the roller rink, I did not seem to go there much either. The roller rink seemed to come alive on weekends. In the summer, they could open the side windows and let the warm summer breezes blow through, there was no central air conditioning then. They would have all types of "skating"; singles, couples, families, ladies choice, men's choice, and free style. I was not the best skater, but I did enjoy cruising around the rink and watching the better skaters, skate backwards, spin, and do other fancy moves on their skates. For some reason, all the town punks liked to come there. They were good skaters and seemed to delight in harassing those of us who struggled to keep our legs under us. I suppose that is one of the reasons I didn't go there much, too much of the wrong crowd hanging out and causing problems.

Before I was old enough to do some of the more physical farm work or I could drive and go to town, I had to find things on or near the farm to amuse myself. Television might be an hour out of each day for things like Howdy Doody and Captain Kangaroo and that was in black and white. I enjoyed doing things outside like fishing in one of our small creeks, building tree houses, playing in the hay mow, and any other activity that could keep me busy. I loved to take apart things that no longer worked and try to get them to work once again. I was never too successful with that and I guess that is why I did not become a mechanic.

We had two small creeks that ran through our property. It was great fun to dig up some earthworms and head down to the creek and try our luck. I liked going to the "north" creek best because there were some large trees that lined the banks. It was a lot more comfortable in the hot summer to drop your line in the shade of a big cottonwood tree, than sit out in the open sun. We certainly did not have very sophisticated fishing gear. I can remember many times cutting a 4 foot branch off a maple tree to use for a pole. We would tie some fishing line to it, attach a hook, and a bobber and we would be all set. We would try to find a spot in the creek where it had carved out a deeper hole to drop our lines. The creeks were only a matter of inches deep except the "fishing hole" areas. Late in the summer and if the rains were not plentiful, these creeks became mere trickles of water. In Iowa, and in small creeks, you were happy to catch whatever went after your worm. We did not catch bass, or walleye, or northerns. We caught large minnows that we called "chubs" and also fish called "bullheads". I don't really know if there is a fish called "bullheads" or they were just very small catfish. Whatever we caught, we kept in a large bucket of water. After we were done fishing, we would haul or catch back to the farmstead and put these fish in the large watering tanks the cattle used to drink out of. I am not sure why we did that, but it was like having a very large aquarium. The grain that fell off the mouths of the cattle seemed to provide for the nutritional needs of the fish. It seemed that slowly the fish would die off and float to the top. As the number of fish dwindled, we had a reason to make another fishing trip to replenish the tank.

If the fish did not bite, there were other activities to do at the creek. We would look for frogs amidst the weeds at the water's edge. They were very difficult to catch as they could jump fast and far and would often dive into the deeper water and could not be found. Just wading in the small creek was refreshing, particularly if it was a very hot day. That usually resulted in leeches attaching to our feet as we plodded through the muddy creek beds. These leeches were not usually discovered until we got back to the house. Us kids would pretty well freak out when we found them. Mom would have to come to our rescue and extract these gnarly creatures from between our toes. Because our creeks were very small, there was no one area where they were really deep to form a "swimming hole". We always wanted Dad to build a farm pond and stock it with good fish and have a place to swim. That was never one of his priorities however and we were all much safer because we did not have a farm pond.

It was also fun just to play in the water. We would throw rocks into the deeper pools; look for artifacts like arrowheads; and build little dams and waterfalls. I am not sure what the fascination with those little creeks was all about, but we did log many hours and they sure helped pass the time away.

One activity I enjoyed also was building "clubhouses" and "tree houses" and then using these small sanctuaries to escape. Our clubhouses were built in the trees away from the house and other out buildings on the farm. In the summer, when the trees were leafed out and the weeds grew up around them, they seemed like secluded hideouts miles from civilization. They were pretty crude structures. They were made of old posts and scraps of lumber cobbled together to form a one room shanty. The roof was old pieces of tin, and certainly not water tight. The inside of the clubhouse walls were covered with discarded paper feed sacks. They covered all the cracks in the walls and made the clubhouse light tight. We would salvage just about anything we could for furniture; old buckets, wooden crates, and the like. A table could be any wide board held up by two cream cans or buckets. I really can't recall what we all did inside those shanties. It was quite dark inside these little shacks, so we used kerosene lamps and candles for lighting. We were very fortunate the clubhouse itself never caught on fire, it would have probably have gone up in smoke in a matter of seconds. I think it was just the idea we could escape the watchful eye of our parents for a brief time and we could pretend we were in the deep woods with all kinds of wild creatures just outside our door.

I also remember a tree house that I built in the grove of trees behind our house. I think every boy dreams to have a tree house and I was no different. My dad was quick to point out that we did not really have the right trees to build a tree house. The ideal tree for a great tree house has to be a very large, old tree, preferably an oak. It should have a large trunk and 10-15 feet above the ground it should have several large branches that fan out in several directions. It is at this point you can place the bottom of your tree house and then build the side walls and roof. We just did not have trees like that on our farmstead. However, I was not deterred. In the far corner of the farmstead were two large maple trees which were tall and straight. I found an old discarded telephone pole that was in good shape. I dug a hole in the ground and stuck this pole in the ground so that it formed one point of a triangle with the two maple trees. I then used 2 x 4's to connect the two trees and the pole about 10 feet above the ground. I then laid boards across the 2 x 4' to form the floor of the tree house. I went up about six feet and connected the top of the pole with the two maple trees. I laid boards on top of these to form the roof of the tree house. I used other boards to cover the sides. It was a cool tree house. It was shaped like a triangle and it was 10 feet above the ground. I nailed wooden slates to the pole so that I could easily climb the pole to get into the tree house. I mounted an old hay rope pulley in the back of the tree house with a rope through it. There was a five gallon bucket attached to the rope that we used to hoist things up to the tree house. It was a tree house that was the envy of the neighborhood. It was large by most tree house standards, so 5-6 people could easily be inside at one time. Many good times were had by all. Once in a while, a curious squirrel or blackbird would poke its head through a window, but would depart quickly when they saw humans occupying the space. That old tree house survived for a long time after I out grew it, but eventually it was gone as the old trees were cleared and new pine trees were planted in their place.

As I mentioned in an earlier section on the farm buildings, the barn was a source of entertainment. It was a great place for the neighborhood kids to get together. When the hay loft was full of hay and straw, we would build tunnels through the straw. These tunnels were made by laying the bales end to end and two bales high and parallel to each other. Another bale was placed across the top of the bales to create the tunnel effect. They were quite narrow, so you could just barely squeeze down through them. They were also light tight as well, which helped create a very scary environment. It was also important to create a "room" so that several people could be together. This required a little bit of mechanical knowledge and imagination. Two by fours had to be used across the top of the stacked bales so a room could be made. These tunnels were great places to play hide and seek. The rooms were also places to gather with friends and talk about the important things in life. We were smart enough not to use matches, candles, etc. One little slip and the whole barn would be in flames. We borrowed a few flashlights to illuminate our way. You would be a little nervous to be the first in the tunnels, especially if you had not been in them for a while. You could never be certain that a feral cat, raccoon, or opossum might have decided to take up living quarters in the tunnel. The first one in the tunnel had the biggest flashlight and made the most noise, hoping to drive out any unwanted occupants.

Another fun activity in the hay mow was swinging on the hay rope and then dropping into a big pile of straw. This is the same principle as tying a rope to a tree branch and then swinging out over a pool of water and then dropping into the water. In our case, we had to secure the rope to the peak of the barn roof, this was no easy task. On one side of the barn, we would stack bales as high as we could for our launching platform. Opposite from the stack of bales we would mound up a big pile of straw from broken bales. It was great fun to climb to the top of the stack, grab a hold of the rope and launch yourself toward the pile of straw. At the right time you would release from the rope and drop into that soft pile of straw. Your timing had to be perfect. If you held on too long, you might collide with the barn wall; if you let go too soon, your landing could be on a pile of bales, or even worse, the floor of the hay mow. Surprisingly, there were very few injuries; a few scrapes and bruises, but no concussions or broken bones.

As the hay and straw were used, the hay mow floor eventually became bare. With a little extra work, a large area could be cleared to make a small basketball court. We mounted a basketball hoop on one of the large oak cross beams to complete the process. We also mounted some portable lamps to the rafters so we could play at night as well. My brother liked basketball more than me, but it was fun to have friends over and shoot a few hoops. You could play basketball rain or shine, day or night, and not have to run into town to do that. As you can see our old barn was very functional, but also provided some extracurricular activities for the kids as well.

I am not sure how this activity got started, but the older kids in the neighborhood decided it would be fun to get together on the weekends with our horses. I would say there was probably a total of 10 families represented at these gatherings. Each weekend, we would meet at someone's house and then just ride our horses around. Often times there would be two riders for each horse. We would try to go to areas where we could "explore" the area. We could not go into the fields of corn, soy beans, or hay, but pastures, and wooded areas around creeks were great. We were supposed to stay on our own property, but some of the best riding areas were in our neighbor's fields. One such neighbor was Bill Holst. He was a grumpy, somewhat reclusive individual that just wanted to be left alone. He had a wonderful creek pasture and one Saturday, it was just begging to be explored. His farm was not too far from ours; in fact one of the little creeks that meandered through our farm went immediately into his ground. There must have been about 8-10 horses that day and about 20 neighborhood kids. We were having a great time until Bill spotted us. He came out to the creek where we were hanging out and wanted to know what we were doing on his property. He promptly told us to get off his land if we didn't want trouble. He was pretty scary, so we decided to heed his advice and get the heck out of there. We thought the next time, he might greet us with his shotgun. In order to leave his ground, we needed to cross that small creek. For some reason, one of the horses decided they were not going to go through the water one more time. We tried many tactics, but nothing was going to convince that horse to cross the water. We finally blind folded the horse, led it away from the water, and then led it as fast as we could back to the water and it plodded through. We eventually made it back to the gravel road that led back to our farm. Dad met us at the road. It seems he picked up the phone to make a call. We had a party line those days and Bill Holst was on our party line. He heard Bill talking to the sheriff about a bunch of ruffians who were on his land destroying his property and harassing his sheep. Needless to say, we all beat a very hasty retreat to our farm. I think the sheriff eventually showed up and asked us politely not to ever go back on Bill's farm. We had no problem with that.

As I said earlier, when you were young and on the farm you had to create your own entertainment. Mom and dad were usually busy doing the farm work. Mom would try to include me in some of her activities if she felt I couldn't do too much damage. This included some garden chores, helping with the chickens, and a little yard maintenance. We also had a few yard toys such as tire swings, a sand box, and of course tree climbing. Of course, there was always a little more to do if the neighborhood kids came over. Certainly, as I got older dad found more and more things for me to do. Entertainment became farm chores and field work.

The Neighbors

There was a real sense of family in rural Iowa and there was also a real sense of community as well. You certainly knew your neighbors and in many cases would often times work with them to complete projects that would be difficult to complete doing them yourself. I alluded to this earlier in the "seasons" portion of this book. Dad worked very closely with his cousin Erv and another neighbor Henry. They seemed almost as much apart of our family as my mom, dad, and siblings. Dad and mom knew not only their immediate neighbors, but also many people in the community and county. They spent most of their lives in Benton County and they both were very active in civic, community, and church work. This was a time when if your neighbor was in need, neighbors, community, and church were there to give a hand. No one went without food, shelter, or clothing, it would not have been right. Like in many small towns, it was difficult to keep secrets. It seemed on several occasions, your neighbors knew more about your business than you did. As in any situation there are positives and negatives and you must deal with what is going on in the present.

For the most part we knew our neighbors and they were good people. They were outgoing, friendly, and if you needed a hand, they were there to help. We had a few reclusive types that wanted to stay to themselves and everyone honored their requests. Even though they were not well known, they were not mean spirited, hated the people around them, or tried to cause problems. They just wanted to be left alone.

One such family was the Groverts. They were a family of two brothers and two sisters, none of whom had ever married. They owned a great deal of land in our county. The two brothers farmed some of their ground, but the sisters rented out their land to local farmers. One of the sisters, Delia, owned 80 acres directly across the road from us. Delia lived in town, but from time to time would drive out and spend a day or two in the country. I assumed this was her way of "getting away" and "roughing it" a bit. The farm house, directly across the road from us, had no electricity, no indoor plumbing, and no means of heating other than a pot bellied stove. She drove a 1939 black Chevrolet. She always wore dark clothing, and wore a big wide black straw hat. I only saw her face to face once or twice. She would pull into the farmstead driveway, open the gate, drive in, close the gate, and then disappear into the house. Once in a while she would be puttering around outside pulling weeds and straightening things up a bit. Since there was no electricity in the house, things were dark inside at night. You could sometimes see a faint glow coming from one of the windows, which we assumed was a kerosene lamp or candle. None of us kids were brave enough to go over and peer through the windows. We would dare and double dare one another to go over and have a peek, but could never muster enough courage to do so. The kids were convinced she was up to sinister purposes. This certainly was not the case, because she was a kindly person and never threatened any of us.

One of the few times I saw her face up close was when she came over to visit with my Dad. When I saw her slowly coming across the road, all kinds of thoughts ran through my head as to what was going to happen. She told dad there was a foul odor coming from her basement and would dad come over and investigate the situation. She was elderly and somewhat frail. I don't think she wanted to navigate the steep narrow steps to the basement and was a little apprehensive as to what might be down there. Dad agreed to help out and I went along. I was not about to miss an opportunity to get inside that house in daylight, no matter what might be in the basement. Delia led us slowly back to her house and to the basement stairs. She gave us a flashlight and we slowly descended the stairs. There was a God awful stench coming from the basement. My imagination was again running wild. I was convinced we were going to find the body of a small child she had tortured to death. What we found however was the decaying body of a large raccoon. Dad and I immediately turned around and headed back up the steps. Dad told Delia what we had found. Well it seems that on her last visit to the country, she heard something in the basement, and threw some rat poison down the steps. That poor raccoon ate the bait and then assumed room temperature. Dad then found a large shovel and a bushel basket and headed back down to remove the decaying remains. I declined to go with him this time as he retrieved the critter. I was not sure I made the right choice however, because I had to spend the next few minutes alone with Delia. We did go outside as the smell was permeating the whole house. I figured if she tried anything, I was younger and faster, and could go screaming home if I had to. She was very grateful to dad and offered to pay him a little something for his trouble. Of course, he declined. I can't say that was the start of a wonderful friendship between a reclusive old lady and a young farm boy, but it did alter my perspective of her. I remember that in future visits if I was in the yard when she pulled in the driveway across from us, she would give a gentle wave or I would see a gentle smile from beneath that broad brim of her straw hat. I did not look at her with the distrust I had in the past. Eventually, Delia's health declined and she quit making those trips to the country. I also remember hearing the news that she had passed away as well. Sort of sad in a way, that what seemed like such a pleasant gentle lady passed on with so few people knowing or caring.

Delia was certainly the exception rather than the rule of our neighbors. I could not possibly list them all and tell you about them that would be several books in and of itself. I will mention a few and what made them special to me. To our immediate south were the Inmans. Myron and Flossie were the parents. They seemed elderly at the time. Their youngest son, Roger, was a little older than my oldest brother. Their middle son, Richard, was married and lived on the same farmstead as they did. Their eldest son, Robert, was killed in WW II during the D day invasion. They were small in stature, but had large hearts of gold. They were good Christian people and I can never remember hearing a harsh word coming from their mouths. They always seemed interested in what you were doing, but were not snooping or prying. Richard eventually left the farm and moved away to another avocation. Roger married and he and his wife and their family lived on the home farmstead. Myron passed away and left Flossie alone. She remained on the farm well into her 80's until health issues forced her into a care facility. Flossie was truly one of a kind. You would have been unable to guess her age, her smooth complexion, the twinkle in her eye, and a pleasant smile made her look years younger than she was. She made you feel good just being around her. In the care facility, she took it upon herself to be the goodwill ambassador. She was so kind to mom in her final months in the home. We all felt Flossie would live forever, but unfortunately she fell ill in her mid 90's and passed away. What a treasure lost!!! She truly lived life to its fullest. Never complaining about life's valleys and always trying to help her fellow man.

In contrast to the Inmans, were the Schwartz's. Al and Shirley had three daughters and a son. They always seemed to be trying to win life's lottery and usually failing. While most neighbors would be willing to work with one another, the Schwartz's liked doing things on their own. They liked to talk and loved to spread the neighborhood news, good or bad. Their language would make a sailor blush and at times in the still of the evening you could hear them yelling around the farmstead. Dad and Al were always friendly to one another, but neither dad nor mom ever became close friends with them, just neighbors. In the summer, you could usually count on the Schwartz's for a little entertainment in the evening from time to time. We affectionately called their evening antics the Schwartz rodeo. Like most farmers then, the Schwartz's had their share of pigs and cattle. From time to time, critters would escape from their designated quarters or pasture and would then need to be rounded up and returned to their proper spot. Out west, a horse would be used to round up the cow or pig, for Al, the pickup truck was the best way to accomplish this. If a cow was in the wrong pasture, Al would chase that cow with his pickup. The cow was usually scared to death of the large pickup bearing down on its backside. It would run and buck and try to jump out of the way, and rarely understood where it was supposed to go. As the chase ensued, Al would become increasingly frustrated that the cow would not immediately run back to its pen. He would be honking the horn and yelling out the window, confusing the cow even more. From time to time the cow was unable to dodge the pickup and Al would bump its back side, causing it to bolt out of the way or be knocked to the ground. Eventually, the cow would tire and give up and finally head back to its pen. Returning an errant hog to its pen required a little different approach. Al would still use his pickup, but if the pig was not too large, he would chase it for a while with his pickup until it began to tire. He would then pull up along side the hog, slam on the brakes, jump out of the pickup, chase the pig, and then try to tackle it. This was always great fun to watch since the pig could usually out maneuver Al for a while. Eventually, he would capture the pig and he would haul it squealing at the top of its lungs back to the pickup. He would throw it in the back and then transport it back to its pen.

I don't recall all the details of what happened, but one time several head of his cattle had broken out of their pen and headed for a cornfield. It was later in the summer and the corn was 6-7 feet tall. The cattle could easily hide in the tall dense foliage of the corn field. He did call over and ask if we would help. We had a large "riding" mare and wondered if we would ride her over, as we would be able to better spot the cattle amongst the corn. My brother and I headed over immediately on our horse, because we knew this would be quite an exciting event. Al and Shirley were raising ponies at the time and Al had decided he would ride up and down the corn rows on one of his Shetland ponies. Al was not a tall man and he had a portly frame. When he perched himself on top of the pony, he probably was shorter than if he walked. I am sure the pony would have preferred he walked as well. The pony had all it could do to trot up and down the corn rows carrying Al on its back. I can remember riding our mare in those cornfields and seeing Al bouncing up and down on that pony a few rows over. You could only see Al and it was as if you were watching the Pillsbury Doughboy jumping through the corn on a pogo stick. You could hear the rustling of the corn as the errant cattle ran ahead of us. You could also hear Al cursing the pony as it was bouncing him all over and hear him cursing the cattle that were running up ahead. It was all I could do to stay on our mare as I was laughing so hard at "bouncing" Al. It was probably more by luck than skill that the errant cows were chased out of the cornfield and returned to their pasture. The memories of cowboy Al have remained a long time.

The nightly rodeos were only one of the many ways the Schwartz's provided entertainment. It seemed whatever activity they got involved in, you could count on something going awry and their reaction always unpredictable. It was like having Laurel and Hardy living next door.

One our closest neighbors were Erv and Dorothy Happel and their two sons John and Jim. Dad and Erv were first cousins, Erv's mother, Katie, and dad's father, Martin, were brother and sister. Dad and Erv grew up together and at times they lived several miles apart, but we always did a lot of farm work together, hay and straw baling, and harvesting corn in the fall. Erv and dad were about the same height and build, but did not look that much alike, but I am sure many would have thought they were brothers. You could always count on Erv to have a smile on his face and a story or two to tell. He had a very distinctive laugh that just made you feel good all over when you heard it. He was always willing to help dad, or anyone else, when needed. I am not sure if "no" was in his vocabulary. Dorothy was also very jovial. She had a smiling face and wonderful complexion. She was a great cook and was always battling a weight problem. Heart and blood pressure problems led to her premature death. John was my age and we did many things together, church, school, 4-H, etc. We remained very close until after high school. John relocated to the Seattle area and I only saw him a handful of times after we graduated from high school. He was a strong strapping type of guy and it was a big surprise when he died suddenly of a heart attack in his early fifties. Jim was John's younger brother. They seemed to bug one another as brothers often times do. Jim grew up married and had two sons and continues to farm only a short distance from where he grew up. Katie, Erv's mom, was quite a lady. Her husband died when he was quite young. Rather than stay alone, she would spend a few months at each of her four children's homes. We got to see "Aunt Katie" as we called her, quite a bit when she stayed with Erv and Dorothy. I can not remember her not having silver grey hair. She was short in stature, but as feisty a woman as you ever saw. She loved to joke and kid and when we were small, she would wrestle with us or play any game we could think of. She loved to cook and she loved to take care of the garden. Even on the hottest of summer days she would be in the garden hoeing, pulling weeds, or harvesting some delicious home grown vegetable. Like many farm women she could whip up a delicious meal and not bat an eye. One of my favorites was her homemade, hand squeezed lemonade. That was always a big treat when we baled hay at Erv's when Aunt Katie brought out her ice cold lemonade. She would usually serve it in the middle of the afternoon when we took a "lunch" break. It tasted so good and it seemed to have magical powers to refresh a tired body. Along with the lemonade, Aunt Katie would serve a story or two as well; she had a great sense of humor. She also loved the 4th of July. While all the other ladies were in the house preparing the food, she would be outside playing with fire crackers. One of her favorite tricks was to light a string of 20-30 small firecrackers and then throw them at our feet. She would nearly bend over with laughter as the firecrackers were jumping all over the ground and we would be jumping as fast as we could away from them. I know she had more fun than we did. Katie remained strong and active for many years. She even cared for her daughter when she fell victim to a stroke. Eventually she ended up in a care facility where she slowly faded away; I believe she lived to be over 100 years. Another wonderful treasure lost. The Happel's were by far our closest friends. When dad died, I can remember Erv writing he had lost his very best friend in a sympathy card. Erv lived into his 90's and his passing was a sad moment for our family.

Although not a neighbor in the sense that he and his family lived near us, Dick Crump, was a good friend and a neighbor in every sense of the word. Dick was a livestock feed salesman for the Moorman Manufacturing Co. He and his wife Dixie lived in the town of Vinton and I believe they had three children, two boys and a girl. If you were a farmer, there were a myriad of sales people that would call on you for all the products you used on the farm; livestock feed, fertilizer, seed corn, farm equipment, trucks, farm buildings, and ad infinitum. Dad was no different and many a salesman stopped by to see dad. There were some he would barely give the time of day, there were others dad liked and would visit with them. However, I believe Dick was probably his favorite. Dick was a young man when he began calling on dad. Trust me; dad was not always easy to deal with. Dick was persistent, very persuasive, honest, and trustworthy; very much a man of his word. These qualities meant a lot to dad. Dick would stop in about every two weeks and take dad's order for the feeds that he needed. Although dad did not like to have his day interrupted, he always seemed find time to visit with Dick. Dick was one of the few salesmen that were ever invited in the house to have some coffee and some homemade apple pie. Eventually, Dick was promoted to a higher management level and moved away from Vinton. I know dad was very disappointed to see him leave town. Dick and his family remained in contact with mom and dad over the years. When mom passed away, Dick took the time to write a letter to us, the children, about how he felt about mom and dad. They were very special thoughts and comments that showed just how special his friendship was to our family. Dick and his family will always be remembered as very special people.

As I said earlier, I could write volumes on the good decent people we considered neighbors. Most all of them were farmers. All of them worked hard to provide for their families. They had a deep sense of caring for their families, their immediate neighbors, and the people in their churches and communities. They truly defined what rural America was all about during that time. As time rolled on, the number of farms has diminished as well as the number of people making their livelihood on the farm has declined. A square mile of land that once had 3-4 families might now only have one and that family may not be engaged in farming, but rather living in the country and working in town. Like so many "mom & pop" institutions, the small family farm has disappeared and has been replaced by the large corporate entity. Those families that remain in the country and derive their livelihood from farming are still "salt of the earth" people, it is a shame their numbers are becoming so small.

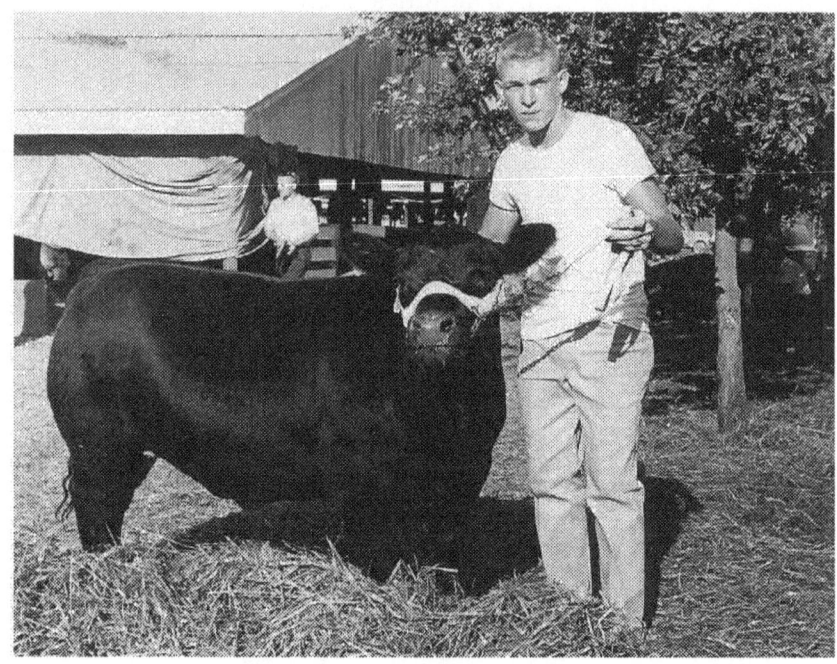

Gene with His 4-H show steer 1964

Benton County Fair Grounds

The Cattle Barns on the Fair Grounds

4-H & the County Fair

If you were a young farm lad or gal in Iowa, there was a very good chance you would belong to one of the local 4-H clubs. I am not entirely sure of its origin, but it was supported very heavily by the local county extension office and Iowa State University. The 4 "H's" came from the words; head, hands, heart, and health.

You had to be at least 10 years old to belong to a club. Each county had several clubs, usually based on one club per township. We lived in Eden township in Benton County. Because our township was well populated, we had two 4-H clubs, North Eden and South Eden. Our club was called the "North Eden Blue Racers". We were racing for the blue ribbons at the county fair. I know I was very excited when I turned 10 years old and could start going to the 4-H club meetings. My good friends, John Happel, Dean Schminke, Keith Geiken, and Doyle Sanders also turned 10 and joined the club as well.

Meetings were held once a month in one of the member's homes. Our club leaders were fathers of the members. I should add that back then, there was boy's 4-H clubs and girl's 4-H clubs, but girls could belong to the boy's 4-H club if they wanted to. I don't know of any boys that were in the girl's 4-H club. Each club would have officers and different activities would occur at every meeting. The main purpose of the clubs was to teach responsibility and be good citizens, much like the boys and girls scout clubs. The farm

moms would usually prepare some delicious snacks to consume
after the meeting.

Each club member was required to have a project for the year.
When I first joined, most of the projects were raising livestock.
As the years progressed, projects included a variety of things such
as raising grain, engine repair, and other academic endeavors. My
older brother, Roger, was also in 4-H at that time and we usually
chose beef cattle as our project. Each member was responsible for
acquiring an animal, up to three was allowed, raising it, caring for
it, and training it, so you could exhibit that animal at the county
fair, held in early August every summer. Depending on the animal
and your training, you could win a blue, red, or white ribbon at the
fair. Everyone of course, wanted to win a blue ribbon. You also
sold your steer at auction on the final day of the fair to bring your
project to a conclusion.

Shortly after the fair in August, you needed to start looking
for your next year's animal. Most of the time, dad would tell the
local sale barn to keep their eye's open for some animals suitable
for 4-H projects. We would drive to the sale barn located on the
edge of town and look at 20-30 steers mulling about in a large pen.
My first year in 4-H, I picked only one animal to look after, but in
subsequent years, I would have two or three steers as my project.
Although I would be in the pen looking, ultimately dad would
make the choice since he certainly had far more experience than
me. After we had made our selections, we would sort them out,
load them on the truck, and haul them home.

Because these were 4-H calves and because we were supposed
to provide all their care, these calves were kept separate from
the other cattle we had on the farm. The one side of our big old
barn was used for very little, so that became the home of our 4-
H projects. They had nice warm shelter in the winter and a small
exercise area outside with a watering tank. It was my responsibility
to make sure they were properly fed and watered. I also had to
insure they had clean, dry, bedding. Most of the time they were
looked after in the morning after the cows were milked and in the
evening before the cows were milked. Their pens were normally

cleaned on the weekends when there was more time. One of the goals of raising beef cattle was to have them gain weight quickly, efficiently, and be a fine specimen for butchering when all was said and done. You were always trying to come up with the right blend of grains, hay, and concentrates to accomplish this goal. All the feed salesmen tried to convince you their supplements were the best. They also had some "secret" recipes to add to the diets to make your steer do the best. It did not take me long to figure out that genetics were far more important than the supplement you fed. The better quality animal you picked was the secret, as long as it got a good diet.

Caring for the animal was part of the project. Keeping records for food consumption, costs for feeding and caring for the animal, weight gain, and feed efficiency were also a big part of the project. In other words, were you making any money with this endeavor? Shortly after the new year started, all project animals had to be weighed. The animals had to be loaded up and taken to town for the official "weigh in". This was your base line to measure how your animal did, because it would be weighed again at the start of the fair. I believe your steer had to weigh at least 400 pounds but could not weigh over 600 pounds.

Not a lot was done other than routine care in the winter months. As I said earlier though, these steers were going to be exhibited at the county fair. These animals were not just turned loose in a pen where a couple of judges would look at them and assign you a ribbon. No, these animals had to be led with a harness on their head in a judging arena with 20-25 other steers. They were required to walk around the arena and then placed in several different positions for the livestock judge to examine. So, in the summer, you had to halter train your steer so that it would follow you around and then train it to stand for the judge's examination. Because these animals saw you every day and there was a certain amount of interaction with them on a daily basis, they were a little easier to train, than one of those big strapping steers in the regular feeding lot. However, halter training was not without challenges. These animals were not real fond of you trying to put a leather or rope halter on them and then forcing them to do things that were not real natural. The secret for successful training was starting early in the summer and working slowly with each animal on a daily basis. This rarely happened, at least with me. I would procrastinate most of June and then scramble like crazy in July to get that steer ready for the fair in August. These animals were also groomed as well. Their heads were clipped, their tails and hooves were trimmed, they were bathed weekly, and their hair was brushed and combed to make it soft and shiny. The calves did not mind the cool bathes in the hot summer time however. Most of the time when it was time to go to the fair, the calves were trained enough to go into the show ring. You just hoped and prayed everything would go OK. Your greatest fear was that your calf would kick the judge or that something would spook your animal and it would take off running, dragging you behind it and embarrassing you in front of your friends and their families. Most of the time things went smoothly and your worry was a wasted emotion.

As I mentioned earlier, you could have a variety of livestock products. You could take pigs, dairy calves, sheep, and even chickens to the fair. Beef calves seemed to be the more macho thing to do. At the fair, the beef calves occupied the most space and most of the judging time. The beef barns seemed to be where most of the action was as well. Swine projects required very little effort on the farm or at the fair. You would select 3-4 piglets for your project shortly after they were born. Often they would be raised with the rest of the hogs and maybe a month before the fair you would segregate them to an area of their own. You would work with them using a small wooden panel and they too received a bath periodically. At the fair, you would herd one of the pigs into the arena and work it around so that the pig was always between you and the judge. Each pig was judged on its confirmation and how it would butcher out. A male and a female pig were judged individually, and then the pen of three was judged as a group. Blue, red, and white ribbons were handed out as with the cattle. I did not take any other livestock projects other than cattle and hogs.

Some of my friends took sheep and dairy. I am not sure who took chickens or rabbits.

As I mentioned earlier, we had monthly meetings where we would gather in a member's home. Much of the time was spent discussing the progress of our individual projects. We had project notebooks that had to be updated and then when our project ended turned in for evaluation. Someone would give a brief program pertaining to agriculture and some time was spent planning a few social events. There were softball tournaments, basketball tournaments, hay rides, wiener roasts, and the like that provided some additional entertainment. Most of these were summer time activities as it was just too cold to do anything in the winter outside, other than sledding parties. Certainly once summer arrived, the big focus was getting ready for the county fair.

When you turned 14, you could go to the 4-H summer camp near Madrid, Ia. You did not automatically get to go however, since space was limited for each weekly session, and it was the only 4-H camp for all the 4-Hers in the state. I recall going to camp twice once when I was 15 and I believe the second time I was 17. Camp was a lot of fun. You got to meet people from all over the state. You did lots of typical "camp" activities, swimming, canoeing, crafts, camp fire building, etc. I also remember they had social activities in the evenings as well. These were usually mixers so you could meet other campers and especially meet and dance with those pretty little 4-H gals. Going to 4-H camp was my first experience being away from my family for more than a day. I loved it. No flaming hot relationships developed from those camp experiences, but I did meet and make friends with a lot of guys and gals. The only down side to all of this was the report you had to give to your local club when you got home about all the good people you met, the wonderful things you learned, and the experiences that would stay with you a life time.

Nothing defined the 4-H experience more than the county fair. This became the highlight of the summer for the 4-H kids, their parents, and the community around the fairgrounds. Our fair was the Benton County Fair held in Vinton, Ia., the county seat town.

This barren piece of ground on the southeast edge of town would come alive every year in early August. Although, it was not the largest or the most famous of Iowa County Fairs, it was a very good quality fair. The livestock barns would fill up with cattle, hogs, and sheep. A traveling carnival would setup their rides in the Midway. The local equipment dealers would bring in a variety of farm equipment to show off the latest and greatest stuff. There were a couple of small exhibition halls where local merchants would also setup shop for a few days and try to peddle their wares to the fair goers. The grandstand would come alive at night with a variety of entertainment. Last but not least was the exhibition hall where the more domestic wares were displayed and judged. This included all kinds of fresh produce, baked goods, and a variety of items that showed off the sewing talents of the locals. This small track of land was a buzz with activity. During the day, all the different types of livestock were judged. The cattle were judged in a large fenced arena. Bleachers surrounded the arena so that nervous parents could sit and watch their children demonstrate their showmanship skills. It was also a great place for the adults to sit and carry on endless conversations with their neighbors. The talk often centered on the present crop situation, market prices for livestock, or about some piece of equipment they saw on the fairgrounds. Frequent trips were made to one of the concession stands for refreshments. It got pretty hot during the afternoons in August. The hogs and sheep were judged in a smaller arena that was covered with a large tin roof. Although not as popular a venue as the cattle judging, the shaded arena provided some relief from the hot summer sun or the occasional afternoon thunder shower.

The midway usually opened some time in the afternoon, when the carnival folks had shaken off their hangovers for another day and tried to drum up a little business. The selection of rides was limited in such a small county fair setting. You could usually count on a Ferris wheel, merry-go-round, tilt-a-whirl, scrambler, and small roller coaster. There were also a few "kiddy" rides for the very small youngsters that came to the fair. There were usually a dozen or so tents where you could try and outwit the "carnies" and try to win a stuffed animal. You could usually count on such things as; knock over the milk bottles, break the balloons with darts, ring toss, and some mini rifle range to take some of your hard earned cash. The carnies were very good at persuading you to try your skills. More often than not, their games to test your skills drained your pocket and your prize was some cheap trinket made in Japan. One of my favorite games was the little mechanical crane where you tried to retrieve a prize with the little scoop on the end of the crane. Many times the little bucket failed to grab anything but thin air or as you carefully tried to maneuver your prize to the prize hopper it would fall from the bucket and you would end up empty handed. I think the best I ever did with this game was a small pocket knife. I don't know how much money I invested in those machines getting that one knife, but I probably could have bought 20 knives at the local hardware store for what I spent digging it out of the prize pile with that crane.

In the evening, the midway would come alive. Many of the activities at the fair were over, and many of the town folks would come out to check things out. The carnival rides would go non stop and their brightly colored lights brightened their drab exterior. Loud music would blast from the pole mounted speakers and there was a constant din of carnies begging you to visit their tent. The warm humid summer air was filled with the smell of fried onions, hamburgers, fries, and sausages. There was nothing quite like taking your favorite gal on the Ferris wheel late at night. You would always hope it would stop at the very top so you could give her a hug or a little kiss or just gaze at the sites below. At that time of my life, it did not seem like life could be any better than this.

The midway was one venue that was very active at night, but there was also the grandstand show. The fair lasted four days and there was some type of entertainment that occurred every night in front of the grandstand. The most popular venue was the stock car races that occurred on the ¼ mile dirt track in front of the grandstand. Although this was a far cry from NASCAR of today, it was great entertainment then. It was pretty much some good old boys souping up a beat up car and seeing how they could do against some other good old boys with the same plan. There were several races each night. The evening was not a success without a pile up or two. I don't think anyone was ever hurt, but it sure was fun to see those cars roll over and over with dust and smoke going everywhere. The evening finale consisted of almost every car that was still running and lots of trips around that ¼ mile track. I am sure prizes were awarded, but I don't recall what they were.

A similar type of show involved some very skilled drivers performing stunts with late model cars. These guys would weave their cars in and out in front of the grandstand and never hit one another. They would fly over ramps jumping other cars, jump through rings of fire, or run one set of wheels over a ramp and see how far they could go down the track with two wheels on the ground and two wheels off. They were quite impressive. I remember one such group, Joey Chitwood and his auto daredevils. We never tried to imitate their stunts with our cars or tractors, but we did try some stunts with our bicycles.

The fair board would usually have some other types of entertainment as well. It was a cheesy comedian, band, or variety act and usually not very good. Needless to say the grandstand was not too full on those nights.

Although you could not count on it every year, once and a while there would be a stripper tent in one of the corners of the midway. When the grandstand show was over, when the families had left the fairgrounds the hawker for the strip tent would emerge with his sandwich board and place it firmly in front of small nondescript tent. The hawker would appear on a small platform in front of the tent with his sandwich board announcing the lovely Lucy's eminent arrival. He was your typical greasy character with slick dark hair and flashy clothes. Shortly after he had a crowd gathered in front of him he would bring out the lovely "Lucy". As I recall she was not that lovely nor was she overly endowed. She would dance around a bit in her skimpy, slinky dress; tantalizing all the men and inviting them to come inside the tent if they wanted to see more. She would then slip back into the tent, the hawker would urge everyone to have a closer look, and for a few dollars your evening would be complete. I had seen these all before, but one rule was that you had to be 18 to be admitted. It so happened that only a few days before my last fair, I had turned 18 and I would be allowed to enter the mysterious tent. A number of my friends and cousins had also turned 18 that year. Most of us would not be coming to the fair again as a 4-Her, so we paid our money and went on in. The tent was dimly lit and everyone inside was either smoking a cigar or cigarette. There was a small stage at one end of the tent with a red curtain hanging near the back of the stage. There were no chairs to sit on and the smoke was so thick it was tough to see or breathe. The hawker was very persuasive and within a few minutes the tent was stuffed full of drooling men of all ages. The lights dimmed even further and some multicolored lights illuminated the stage. The music came from a small record player near the corner of the stage. It was loud and the record was scratched, but by this time no one cared. Finally, after much anticipation the lovely Lucy emerged from behind the curtain. She was still clothed in her skimpy outfit, but slowly and in a tantalizing manner removed each piece. Being a naïve farm boy, this was a sight to behold and one that I had not seen before. It wasn't long before she was down to a "g" string and pasties. With a lot of coaxing and a few extra dollars, those were soon lying on the corner of the stage and the lovely Lucy was stark naked in front of us with only her sparkling high heeled shoes on. One of my first cousins was standing in the front row, with his arms crossed, smoking a huge cigar. He appeared very serious except for a small smirk of a smile. I think Lucy was disappointed he was so calm and showing so little emotion. She danced right over in front of him, turned her back side to him, and wiggled her fanny in his face. I saw him take a big draw on his cigar and slowly remove it from his mouth. I wondered what he was going to do now. Just as that thought was entering my mind, he blew all that smoke right at her rear end. Almost like a magnet, that smoke curled up her front and back side, giving the impression that something was on fire. Needless to say the whole place was roaring with laughter. The lovely Lucy hardly missed a beat but her act came to an end all too quickly. We all exited out the back side of the tent hoping no one we knew would be there. I am sure there was another show later on, but I wasn't sure if my heart and lungs could stand it. That evening was certainly a topic of conversation for a long time after that.

I think one of the reasons I enjoyed the fair so much was because I actually got a little vacation from the day to day chores of the farm. If you had a livestock project at the fair, you had to watch over them. To me this was four days at the fairgrounds, taking care of my livestock, and hanging out with my buddies and cousins. I still had to get up early and milk the cows, but then it was off to the fairgrounds and tend to my chores there. As I said earlier, most of the time my projects were cattle. At the fair, they were not loose in pens, but were haltered and tied into place. That meant several times a day they needed to be taken out and exercised, fed, and their bedding cleaned and changed. In the livestock barns, your 4-H club had all of its livestock grouped together. Your individual projects were judged, but your club was also judged on how well it kept its area of the barn clean. Each club would try to have a member or two present at all times to make sure everything was neat and orderly and that manure was picked up and removed promptly. At times, it could get a little boring just hanging out and listening to the radio. Lots of stories were told, and cards were played to help pass the time. When your "watch" was over, you would hit the midway, the other livestock barns, the machinery exhibits, or the judging arenas. Another fun spot to hang out at was the camping area. 4-Hers that lived in the southern part of the county would often pitch tents and stay overnight on the fairgrounds. A number of my cousins did this and they had a large tent that would hold 6-8 cots. There was usually a friendly game of cards going on or some sort of bull session to participate in. You could also count on one or two issues of Playboy magazine being there as well for your gazing pleasure. I usually got out of the evening chore scene. It was also rare that any field work was being done at that time as well. Dad and mom seemed to be content to give us a little space for those few days. As I said earlier, there were a number of concession stands around for food and snacks. However, a real treat was when mom would make a picnic lunch and bring it in. Early August was a time when a lot of fresh produce was in season. She would usually make some meat sandwiches, but then bring in tons of sweet corn, tomatoes, green beans, peas, and of course watermelon. It was truly a gorge yourself fest.

With all of these activities going on, sometimes you lost sight of the fact that you had your livestock project to show and compete with the other projects at the fair. Judging beef cattle was usually an all day affair, as there were usually so many. The individual classes were based on the breed of cattle, i.e. Angus, Hereford, shorthorn, etc. and also by weight, i.e. light weight, middle weight, heavy weight, and the like. The day of the show, you had to make sure your steer got a bath and you fussed with it until it was ready for the show ring. For the real pros, the hooves were covered with black shoe polish, the tail was fluffed and ratted, skin preparations were applied to the hair, and the hair was often "blow" dried to make it look its very best. I just never really got that carried away with the grooming part; I was more worried about how my steer was going to behave in the ring. When your time came to show your steer, you would put on a fancy show halter. We usually showed Black Angus steers, so we would use a very nice, all white halter. It was a sharp contrast on those jet black animals. Everybody in an individual show class would have to line up outside the ring. Like a lot of events, I think the parents sitting on the bleachers were more nervous for their children than the kids were for themselves. When the class ahead of you was done, you paraded your animal in the ring. The judge would usually stand in the center and everyone would walk their steers past him. You would then have to stop and line up all the steers in a row. He would then come down, look each animal over, and in some cases run his hands over the animal. It was when he was checking each animal you prayed that your critter would hold still. You could bet you would not do well if your animal was jumping around or God forbid the judge would get kicked. Most of the time my steer behaved well. Every now and then, some unruly steer would decide to make an early exit. I always felt sorry for the person with that steer and so appreciative it did not happen to me. Once the judge had looked over the class, he would then begin dividing them up into the "blues", "reds" and "whites". Once again, your heart was pounding hoping you would be in that elite blue class. Once the classes were decided, the judge would then try to sort the class in order of best to worst. Normally, my critters were blues and reds, but I had a few whites. These were good lessons in life, i.e. some winners some losers, and the better prepared you were, the better you did. A big sense of relief came over you as an assistant to the judge handed you your ribbon and you could head back to the barn. There was always some discussion as to why you should have done better or the judge was biased towards such and so. It was over, however, and that was great. If you had other steers, you then had to scramble to get them ready and the process was repeated. If you had the time, it was fun to go sit in the bleachers and watch your buddies show their steers and watch them sweat a little as well. When the judging was done, you really felt a sense of relief and you felt very good.

The fair concluded with an auction. Part of the whole project was to sell your steer and see if all of your hard work resulted in a profit. This could be a fairly sad day if you made your project more like a pet. Once again, each animal was taken into the ring and bidders would purchase your steer. All of them ended up going to the packing plant and eventually on someone's dinner table. It was something I tried not to think about. Dad would remind me that we were livestock farmers and that we were raising livestock to sell as meat animals. It was still hard to do, but the check that came in the mail for the sale of my steer did help ease the pain. That money went into a savings account and was eventually used to pay college expenses.

Some today would look at the fair experience as a fairly simple, non exciting event, but for me it was something I looked forward to every summer and enjoyed a great deal. There are 99 counties in Iowa and I believe everyone had a county fair at that time. There were also larger fairs such as the All Iowa Fair in Cedar

Rapids, and the Dairy Cattle Congress in Waterloo. However, the grand daddy of them all was the Iowa State Fair in Des Moines, Iowa's capital city. This was a huge event back in the fifties and remains a big attraction today; it usually runs about 10 days. If you exhibited livestock there, they had to be exceptional; it was the best of the best, so to speak. Everything about the Iowa State Fair was big. There was a huge midway, hundreds of exhibitors, talent shows, variety shows, and usually entertainment that was first class. You could probably spend three or four days there and not see it all. I only went to that fair twice as a youth; once with the family for the day and once with my neighbor John Happel when he exhibited hogs our last year in 4-H. The state fair is truly one of those events you must experience to appreciate, reading about it or seeing pictures of it, just does not capture the essence of the event. It remains today, the epitome of Iowa agriculture. I hope everyone who reads these stories has had or will have a chance to attend the Iowa State Fair.

Benton County Courthouse

Friday Night in Vinton

In the fifties, most of your shopping was done in your local community. As dad would say if they don't have it in Vinton, you probably don't need it. He was a firm believer in supporting the local merchants. Occasionally, we would drive to Cedar Rapids to shop; my mom and sisters did not necessarily agree with dad's credo and felt they had to go there periodically to get those things that were not in Vinton. You also need to understand this was an era when businesses closed at 5 or 6 PM and 99% of them were certainly not open on Sunday. There were no large shopping malls and there was no mentality that you had to be open 24 hours a day, seven days a week.

Our little town of Vinton did have one night a week, however, when the stores stayed open later. That was Friday night and I believe they stayed open till 8 PM for your shopping convenience. This turned out to be quite an event for this rural community, especially in the summer time. The farmers would try to wrap up their field work and chores a little early on Fridays. Everyone would get all cleaned up, put on some decent clothes, pack everyone in the car and head to town. As it turned out, this was more to see who was in town, than it was to do any serious shopping.

In the summer, the high school band would always have band concerts on Friday night. The band would set up on these huge bandstands on big wooden wheels in front of the county

courthouse. Most of the music was the famous "marches" or
a variety of patriotic tunes. The courthouse was located in the
middle of the courthouse square at one end of Main Street. There
was plenty of room to spread blankets on the courthouse lawn or
bring a lawn chair to listen to the tunes. Many others would remain
in their cars with the windows rolled down so they could hear
the music. At the end of each song, every one would honk their
car horns to show their appreciation to the band. A few vendors
would set up shop and sell popcorn, snow cones, or cotton candy.
The music would flow up and down Main Street and you could
certainly hear it for several blocks around the courthouse. Lots of
people would be milling about the courthouse square and up and
down the streets. One year, some pranksters dumped the band
stand in the Cedar River. Fortunately, that did not end the concerts;
they were just moved to a concrete slab adjacent to one of the
school buildings. The music was still good, but it was not quite
the same as it was in front of the courthouse. The young folks that
had driver's licenses would cruise up and down the streets causing
mini traffic jams in our small community. They would be yelling
back and forth to passing vehicles or honking their car horns at one
another. It was like a little mini festival every Friday night in the
summer and truly a slice of rural Americana.

Other activities went on as well. The local theatre, The Palace,
would try to have a good movie playing on Friday nights. When it
was really hot, the community swimming pool was a great place to
cool off and hang out with friends. Before I could drive, the folks
would drop us off at the pool and wait patiently in the car for us to
have our fun. I can not ever remember mom or dad coming into the
pool with us.

One activity that was geared primarily for the teenagers was
square dancing. I am not sure how I ever got started going to this
event, but it was a great time. The square dances were held in the
street adjacent to the Junior High Building. The local police would
block off either end of the block with barricades so we could truly
have a street dance. They would get a professional square dance
"caller" to lead the square dancing. Most of the kids there were

Junior High School students or early High School students. I don't ever recall bringing a date to the dances. You just showed up, paid your dollar and took your chances. The caller would match you up with some gal. You would do a few dances and then you would get another gal. You knew if you didn't get the prettiest one at first you would not be stuck with her for the night. We did have a great time. Everyone there was either friends, neighbors, school mates, or attended your church. The kids had a lot of fun and there was usually a good crowd of parents and curious onlookers that enjoyed watching us go through our paces.

Our Friday night outing, when we were with mom and dad, was usually topped off with a trip to one of the local drive-ins for refreshments or a stop at one of the small grocery stores for ice cream. It was then back home and off to bed. Saturday was no holiday on the farm, but Friday nights in town were a nice break in the routine. As I recall, the local town merchants called this "Friendly Friday" nights.

Small Town Business

One of the things I have missed the most about our small rural town is the businesses and the owners of those businesses. Practically all the stores in the town of Vinton were owned by local people. I do not believe that in the fifties, there was one franchised store in town. Our town had about 5000 people; the surrounding countryside probably had another 1000 people. You did the great majority of your shopping in your home town, so you got to know the stores and their owners quickly. I am not sure that credit cards even existed. You paid your bills with cash or a check. The farm supply stores and hardware stores allowed you to set up a charge account and would send you a bill every month. On Main Street alone you could find the following: two men's stores, two lady's stores, two shoe stores, two hardware stores, two dime stores, two jewelry stores, two drug stores, a small J.C. Penny store, a florist, some professional offices, a photography studio, a movie theatre, some cafes/diners, and furniture stores. There were other shops and stores off main street as well that supplied the other necessities in life. I would like to elaborate on some of them.

One of my favorite stores was Cameron Clothing Company. Cameron's is where dad bought most of his clothes. You could get the whole wardrobe there from dress up to work clothes. You could buy a fine suit or a pair of Osh Kosh by Gosh bib overalls. Dad also bought his dress shoes there as well, but purchased his work shoes at a small Red Wing shoe store and repair shop. I enjoyed going with dad to that store, you were always treated so well. The minute you walked in the door, one of the owners was there to greet you with a big smile, a friendly greeting, and a desire to help you find what you wanted. You were greeted by your first name and taken immediately to the section of the store that you needed. The store was extremely neat and well organized, nothing was out of place. If you were buying a suit or sport coat, they would assist you with putting the jacket on and taking it off. They would not just sell anything for a sale. They wanted to make sure whatever you bought fitted well and you looked good in it. Dad always liked nice suits and at Cameron Clothing if you bought a suit, you got a dress shirt and tie to go with it, at no additional charge. When I was in high school I would often times go in by myself to buy clothes. I always received the royal treatment, just as dad had always received. I guess it really didn't matter; anyone who walked in the door was treated with courtesy and respect. I also remember leaving the store with my purchases and a small slip of paper stating how much money had been put on dad's account.

Across the street and down just a bit was Byrd Hardware. This had to be the classic of all hardware stores. The store was owned and operated by a little man named Byrd. He was small in stature, usually hunched over, and had thinning gray hair that was rarely combed and he had a pair of glasses that slipped down to the end of his nose. This hardware store had three levels, the main floor, basement, and upstairs. The outside of the building had a very weathered paint job and you had to walk up a couple of creaky wooden steps to get in the building. You entered the building through a huge wood and glass door that took a lot of muscle to pull it open. The floors were wood as well and would squeak and creak as you walked about the store. The most commonly needed items were on the main level, finding them was the challenge. Mr. Byrd did not have nice neat aisles where organized shelves displayed the merchandise. Instead, navigating his store was more like navigating a rat maze. Things were stacked here there and everywhere and you were always afraid, you might knock something over as you searched for your goods. It was like a treasure hunt some times looking for that one item you needed only once in a while. Past experience in his store convinced you that what you needed was in the store, you just could not find it. Mr. Byrd would not follow you around, but seemed to have a sense that after so long, you needed some help. He would peer at you over the top of his smudged glasses and yell, "need help?" Once he knew what you were looking for, it was just a matter of following him to the spot. He must have had 1000's of items in that hardware store, but knew the exact location of everyone of them. You always hoped that the item you were looking for would be either upstairs or in the basement. You just did not venture to either of these locations without him being with you. The upstairs and basement were no different than the main floor. Items were stacked all over with seemingly no rhyme or reason. However, Mr. Byrd could lead you directly to what you needed every time. When you had secured all of your products, you would go to the office in the center of the store to pay for your goods. This office was a little world all unto itself as well. It was separated from the rest of the store by a metal cage. Papers, journals and the essentials of running his business were stacked everywhere. There was an old weathered desk in one corner. A little lady, the bookkeeper, sat at the desk shuffling papers and usually mumbling to herself. She had a small desk lamp with an incandescent light bulb to illuminate her work. On an elevated stand stood an old, brass, mechanical cash register. Mr. Byrd would scribble down everything on a small piece of paper, tally up the prices, by hand, no adding machines or calculators back then. If you were paying cash, he would ring up the total on the cash register. It had a magical ring as he hit the last button and the cash drawer would pop open. If you were going to put your items on your account, he would hand the receipt to the bookkeeper, no need to sign any receipts at his place. When I was older and could drive the car, dad would often times send me into Byrd's to get a few supplies. I would just say put it on Raymond's account and he would, no questions asked. He would then stuff everything in a plain paper bag and send you on your way. If he was not too rushed, he would make a little small talk, but he rarely opened up much. He seemed to be a very private man. There was something magical about Byrd Hardware that could never be duplicated.

I don't believe there were any grocery stores directly on Main Street in Vinton. There were two larger stores and several small mom and pop stores scattered around town. Back then, there were no mega supermarkets, at least in Vinton. Even the larger stores were pretty basic in what they offered. They did not have banks, cleaners, floral shops, bakeries, sushi bars, melon bars, inside their walls. Mom liked to shop at Fareway. It was clean and neat and it had everything a rural housewife needed and at a good price. Although, we raised a lot of our own meat, any additional meat was bought at Fareway. They had a long meat counter in the back of the store. The meat was cut up and displayed in a large glass refrigerated cooler across the front of the meat counter. Several butchers were busy in the background cutting and preparing meat. They were always busy, but the minute you stepped up to the counter, they were there to help you. Once again, there was a big friendly smile and a "how can I help you today Louise?". You selected what you wanted and then the butcher would weigh it, wrap in bright white butcher paper and tape it shut. If you wanted something that was not displayed, one of the butchers would get whatever you wanted. He would then use a red grease pencil and write the price and the item on the white paper. He would give you a big "thank you and come again" and send you on your way. The rest of the store was not all that exciting. The produce area was not that large, because so much of what people needed was raised in that area. More exotic items like oranges, grapefruit, bananas, plums, apples, and the like could be found there. I remember mom talking about the prices of things she raised in her garden like green beans and peas, and how expensive they were in the store. At the checkout counter, you were greeted by a friendly face. I did not think too much about it at the time, but some of those checkout clerks had been there a long time. You could count on the same folks being there day in day out year after year. They were always friendly, knew your name, and engaged in a little chit chat as they rang up you purchases on the cash register, no laser scanners then. The groceries were carefully packed away into brown paper bags, no plastic then, and a courteous young guy or gal would help you to your car with your groceries.

There were several mom and pop grocery stores in Vinton as well. They were more on the edge of town and truly were neighborhood stores. They were like the convenience stores of today, but had no gas pumps. They carried a very limited inventory of products and of course they were more expensive than the large stores. They were run by husband and wife teams and most of the time they were in the store; cleaning, stocking, or checking people out. There might also be a high school student assisting with the day to day routines. These little stores slowly faded away. The owners retired or just could no longer compete with the larger stores getting even larger and more price competitive.

As I said before, there were no stores within the grocery stores. I especially remember a small bakery, Ward's, just off Main Street. Because mom was such an excellent cook, she found little reason to go to the bakery, except for getting a fancy cake for a special occasion. Mom could make homemade bread, rolls, pastries, cakes and no one could touch her homemade pies. However, this bakery made some great apple turnovers and doughnuts. The smell of fresh baked goods was overwhelming when you walked in the shop or if you walked by the door when it was open. You were almost compelled to walk in by those fragrant smells. Our junior high school was only 3 blocks away from Wards. It became a favorite spot to frequent over our noon lunch break where we would grab a coke and a frosted doughnut. As junior high students go, we were loud and boisterous and did not spend that much money. I am not sure the owners of the bakery appreciated our business that much and the school discouraged us from going there.

One of the necessities of small town rural Iowa was the "five and dime" stores. I am not sure how this name came about, but I assume it was because originally, most items were 5 or 10 cents. We called them dime stores and we had two of them on Main Street, Fellers and Ben Franklin. These were magical little places

as well. They were the mini K-Marts and Wal Marts of today.
These dime stores carried lots of little items such as; candy,
sewing supplies, school supplies, and the every day necessities
of life. Once again, these were mom and pop businesses where
both husband and wife were in the store working hard every day.
There might be an additional clerk stocking the shelves or assisting
customers, especially during the holiday season. You could always
count on friendly courteous service whenever you walked into
these stores.

Since this was rural Iowa, agribusiness was what made the
wheels turn. In the fifties, there were many small farms around
each of the small towns. In order to operate, these farmers needed
a lot of equipment. They needed tractors, wagons, combines, tillage
equipment, and a variety of tools to make their operations run
smoothly. There were several equipment dealers in Vinton during
the fifties. Every major equipment manufacturer had a dealership
in town; John Deere, International Harvester, Oliver, Ford, Massey
Ferguson, and J.I. Case. They represented the full line of products
their company manufactured plus they would represent other
smaller manufacturers as well that might have a limited line of
equipment. They not only sold new equipment, but they had to
sell repair parts, and offer a repair service as well. Dad seemed
to frequent these places a lot, mainly securing parts to repair or
keep his equipment in shape. He also needed to buy equipment
from time to time as well. I enjoyed going with dad to the dealers,
I had such a curiosity about equipment and gadgets and how they
worked. While he was at the parts department or talking to a
salesman, I would be off snooping around the new equipment. I
would love to crawl up on a new tractor, sit on the seat, and pretend
I was driving it on our farm. I would move the steering wheel and
be pulling on all the different levers. Fortunately, the keys were not
left in the ignition or I am sure I would have tried to start them as
well. There was such a variety of equipment, and I liked to climb
on each piece as if it were a jungle gym. I am sure I drove dad
crazy and the equipment dealers wondered when I would fall off
and break my neck. The repair shop was also an interesting area.

Big tractors were all torn apart, machinery was being welded, and some equipment was being upgraded with newer gadgets to make them work better. Some of those equipment mechanics were worth their weight in gold in what they could do with that equipment.

One other business that should be mentioned was the local sale barn or livestock auction house. These facilities were certainly unique to rural Iowa, yet not every town had one. It was a distribution center for local livestock. It was on the north edge of town. There were a number of outdoor pens, indoor pens, and a small arena with bleachers surrounding three sides of it. Farmers could bring their livestock there to be sold by auction. The animals were herded into the arena and they were sold to the highest bidder. You might sell an individual dairy cow, a group of feeder pigs, a horse or pony, or even some goats. The auctioneer would rattle off his lingo and two men would scan the bleachers for prospective bidders. They would cry out loudly every time someone in the crowd would nod or wave his hand. Dad enjoyed going there to watch the auction. He rarely bought anything, but spent most of his time chatting with other farmers. I got bored after about 15-20 minutes and began to hound dad about leaving. Depending on his conversation, we would either leave or sit there for what seemed like hours. Sometimes to appease me, we would visit the lunch counter inside the sale barn. Here you could get a sandwich, a drink, or a piece of pie. The sale barn would also get in feeder cattle from the western states and sell directly to the farmers. It was definitely a hub of activity and gathering point for the local farm community.

Gene Ski Mask - Christmas, Dad & Verna

Holidays

Back in the fifties, there were only a handful of holidays that were celebrated on a national basis. Unlike today, where there seems to be at least two federal holidays each month.

Most holidays were celebrated with family and in our particular case, with our immediate family and with the Krug side (mom's side) of the family and the Rinderknecht side of the family. We typically celebrated Thanksgiving and Christmas with families. In the summer the 4th of July was celebrated with friends. Other holidays such as Memorial Day and Labor Day were celebrated at home and often times were no different than any other work day on the farm.

Most all of our families were farmers, so getting together was not a real big deal. The Krug side would decide when we would get together and the Rinderknecht side would decide when they wanted to get together. You really didn't have to worry about work schedules; you just planned on not doing a lot of work on the farm that particular day.

Thanksgiving was truly a celebration. Most years with a few rare exceptions, the crops had been harvested and you were getting ready for winter by the time Thanksgiving rolled around. You had a lot to be thankful for at that time of year. Our immediate family would celebrate by going to a Thanksgiving service at our small Lutheran church. Most of the members of the congregation were farmers and often times the sermon was bent towards the completion of another successful growing and harvesting season. The service was held the night before Thanksgiving Day so that you would have the whole next day to celebrate as you chose.

Thanksgiving Day we would get up, do our chores, and then get ready for the big feast. As I recall, some years we would have a big dinner at home, but most of the time we would go to one of the aunt's or uncle's home for the big feast. One year it would be the Rinderknecht side, the next year it would be the Krug side. Having Thanksgiving dinner for your side of the family was no small undertaking. My dad was one of six children; my mom was one of eight children. The fortunate thing was that dinner would rotate to a different house each year. Whoever had the dinner in their home was responsible for the main course, i.e. meat and potatoes, while everyone else would bring salads, appetizers, side dishes, and desserts. Turkey with mashed potatoes and gravy was the standard main course year in and year out. Depending on whose house where the dinner was held, other meat dishes would include, ham, goose, duck, chicken, or roast beef. Salads ran the gamut and each year one of the ladies would try a new one. Depending on the "takers" it would be back next year, or was dropped from the menu. Side dishes were plentiful as well. They included; green beans, baked beans, sweet potatoes, corn, creamed corn, squash, cooked carrots, usually with peas, and a variety of hot casseroles. To top off this bonanza, were a variety of pies, cakes, and ice cream. Pumpkin pie was usually the all around favorite, but you could also expect to see apple pies, pecan pies, cream pies, and a variety of berry pies. Each slice was served with a generous scoop of ice cream or whipped cream. It was not too unusual to make two or three trips back to the food line and you ate until you were ready to explode. Most of the time, you would let the main courses settle for an hour or two and then head back for the desserts later. After the big meal, the men would gather around the black and white TV and catch a pro football game. The ladies of course would clear the tables, clean up the food dishes and wash the dishes. Because these were such huge gatherings, each family would bring their own table service and these had to be also nice and clean before they were packed up to go home.

The weather in Iowa in late November was often times cold, if not just down right nasty. Entertainment after the big dinner usually was inside. As stated before, TV was just coming into its own and the men were fascinated by seeing a pro football game on TV. The ladies would usually engage in small talk after the place was cleaned up. The kids would try to find something to entertain themselves and playing cards was often times the entertainment of choice. Some of the adults would also join in the card games if they had no interest in the TV.

As the afternoon wore down, people would want to leave for home around 4 PM, most had to go home and tend to the evening farm chores, for us it was to milk the cows. Of course, you could not head home hungry, never mind that you had just foundered yourself only a few hours earlier. You could not leave without a snack. That was usually a sandwich, chips, a drink, another piece of pie or some of the leftovers from the big dinner.

This same scenario was repeated every time the relatives got together to celebrate. At Christmas, you would set aside one day for the Krugs, one day for the Rinderknechts, and then Christmas Eve and Christmas Day was celebrated in your own home.

In the summer, you would try to have a reunion on each side at least once. Instead of going to someone's home, you would have a picnic at one of the small town parks. That way, there was some playground equipment for the kids, a small ball diamond for the men to play softball, a horseshoe pit, and a park shelter were the picnic dinner could be set up. We also had a relative who had a home along one of the Iowa rivers. He would host a reunion there every few years. That was always fun because you could explore the trails running through the woods. However, the river was just to muddy and dirty to swim in. I remember one reunion we had at his place. The ladies had set up all the food on some large picnic tables outside. One of the distant cousins, who was an extremely large lady, sat on the bench with her legs facing out instead of under the table. Needless to say, the food on the table did not counter balance her weight on the bench and the table flipped, leaving her on the ground with food all over her and all over the ground. To say she was a little embarrassed would be an understatement. Although a fair amount of food was lost, there was certainly enough on the other tables for everyone. That was a reunion most in attendance never forgot. As with so many large family gatherings, food was certainly the main focus of these summer reunions. We did not do much barbecuing then other than some hot dogs over an open fire. Most of the ladies would bring a hot casserole, a salad, and a dessert. Another big hit in the summer was all the fresh produce from the family garden. There were always lots of fresh radishes, carrots, peas, green beans, tomatoes, and sweet corn. You just could not beat the taste of those home grown vegetables. The desserts were usually made with home grown fruits as well; rhubarb, raspberry, cherry, apple, and peach. Without a doubt, mom made the best apple pie in all of Benton County, if not in the state of Iowa. I don't think there was ever a piece left in her pie pan when we returned home.

Regressing back to Christmas, I would have to say that was one of my favorite holidays. I alluded to this holiday when I spoke about our church. There was a lot of tradition that surrounded this holiday and our family. Christmas eve, we would load up in the car and head to town to our small church for the Christmas Eve service. When we were in Sunday School, we participated in the actual service. Once out of Sunday School you felt a sense of relief that you did not have to perform on Christmas Eve. The church was always decorated for the Christmas season. A very large evergreen tree was decorated and placed in the front of the church. Some greenery was placed around the windows and a large Christmas candle was placed on a shelf between each pair of stained glass windows. Each service was a little different, but the message was always the same, the Christ child came to earth that night for all mankind. One of the most memorable portions of that service was when the offering was taken. This was done after the Christmas program. The candles were all lit, the lights were dimmed, and the street lights on the outside of the building illuminated the stained glass windows. My younger sisters would then play "Oh Holy Night" as a duet on the church's large pipe organ as the offering was collected. Oh Holy night is a beautiful song, but hearing it in that small church, in that setting makes it stick in your mind like no other Christmas song.

After the service, we would pile back into the car and head home. This was always very exciting, because somehow, Santa Claus always knew to come to our house while we were at church for the Christmas Eve service. I can remember coming home one year and a fresh blanket of snow had fallen while we were in church. The moon was shinning brightly as well, making the snow just sparkle. As we stepped out of the car, dad was quick to point out some fresh animal tracks in the snow. He convinced me those were fresh reindeer tracks and once again Santa had been to our house. The kids would dash into the house, throw on the lights, and low and behold there would be presents under the tree. Mom would turn on the tree lights and we would all gather round to open our presents. There was no way we could wait until Christmas morning to open presents. We would each collect our presents from under the tree and when the signal was given, we would start ripping open packages as fast as we could. We would not take turns opening one package at a time; it was more like who could get all of their presents open the fastest. It was 5 minutes of chaos, with ribbons, and paper flying every where. Once the dust had settled, we would gather up our presents and show them to everyone. After that, we would help mom clean up the paper and ribbons. Mom would usually have something hot for us to eat after that, such as chili, soup, or sandwiches. There were also lots of Christmas candies and cookies as well. We all seemed to stay up later than usual on Christmas Eve. If you got toys, it was tough to stop playing with them and go to bed. Eventually everyone retired to bed and just like clock work; dad would be rousting us out of bed at 5:30 in the morning to go milk the cows. No sleeping in late on Christmas Day. I know some years; there was a church service on Christmas Day as well. If we did not have church, we spent the morning checking out our gifts even more. I also believe most years we were at one side of the family or the other to celebrate the holiday, just as we did for Thanksgiving. Depending on who held the Christmas day dinner, the other side of the family would get together another day to celebrate.

Because both of my parents came from such large families, it was impossible to buy gifts for everyone. Both sides of the family were Lutheran and all of the cousins were baptized into the Lutheran faith. We each had God Parents or sponsors, usually the brothers and sisters of mom and dad. The God parents would purchase a gift for each of their God children and would bring it to the dinner. After the big dinner, the cousins would open the presents from their God parents. You received a gift every year until you were confirmed in the church. After that, a card was pretty much it. Getting another Christmas present was usually great fun. I always hoped it would be an exciting gift. Mom always insisted we go thank our sponsors for the presents they gave us. It was tough enough to go thank your aunt and uncle. It was even harder when you had to thank them for those lovely black socks you so desperately needed. Once again, these were huge gatherings with lots of good food and lots of family bonding.

Probably the biggest summer event next to the county fair was the 4th of July. This was more of a celebration with neighbors and friends than with mom and dad's siblings. Fireworks were illegal in Iowa at that time. Some years, someone in the neighborhood would drive down to Missouri and buy a bunch of fireworks and smuggle them back to Iowa. This contraband was nothing big, just lots of firecrackers; small "black cat" finger crackers, cherry bombs, silver salutes, and m-80's. We would also have a few roman candles, sparklers, and some aerial canons. It was lots of fun shooting these off and seeing what damage we could do. We would bury them in the sandbox to explode the sand, or throw them down a post hole driver with a beer can and shoot the can several hundred feet in the air. Thinking back on all the crazy things we tried, I am amazed we did not blow any fingers off or set fire to one of the farm buildings.

It would not have been unusual to work on the 4th of July. This was mid summer on the farm and there might be field work to do, especially if you were behind in some areas. In the evening, we would gather at someone's home to have a picnic supper and then after it got dark watch the local fireworks. Most of the time, these gatherings were in the country at one of the neighbor's farms. It seems to me there were 4-5 families involved. Once again, there was lots of food, especially fresh garden produce, lots of conversation and some means of entertaining the kids. If we had them, we would shoot off the firecrackers. I mentioned in another chapter about Aunt Katie Happel. She loved to light the strings of fifty small firecrackers and then throw them at your feet. She would laugh until you thought her sides would burst as you would run like heck to get away from them. Once it started to get dark, we would load up in the cars and head to Vinton, where there would be a larger fireworks display. At some point, one of the family friends moved to town, near where the fireworks were set off, and we had our annual 4th of July picnic there. That way, we could have our picnic and enjoy the fireworks after it got dark and not have to move to a different location. Although these were not huge events, it was a good time for farm people to kick back and relax for a little bit.

One final point I would like to make. There were lots of opportunities when family and friends got together. Most were celebrating certain events and enjoying each others companionship and friendship. There was always lots of food, fellowship, and fun. Although alcohol was always present, mainly beer, I never recall anyone getting drunk. The men would occasionally have a beer or two and that was it. I look back now and see how totally responsible everyone was. They enjoyed getting together, they enjoyed a beer or two, they did not condemn anyone who did not have a drink, but they did not get carried away and make fools of themselves. They did not endanger themselves, family or friends either by driving home drunk. All the adults certainly set a good example of how to conduct yourself as a responsible adult.

East Elementary - Gene's Grade School Building

School Days for Rog, Verna, Gene - Jolene

School Days 1955 for Rog, Verna, Gene - Jo & Lu

Gene practicing his Coronet

Lincoln Junior High - Gene's Jr. High Schol

Gene with John Happel - H.S. Graduation

Washington H.S. - Gene's High School

Going to School

I wanted to discuss our schools and contrast them to what the school system is today.

Both of my parents attended the one room school house located in the country. They both went to high school, which was located in the closest city. Many people of their generation did not go onto high school. You did not necessarily need that much education if you were going to farm.

The schools I attended were considered very modern in comparison to those my folks attended. When I started kindergarten, I actually went to school in one of those old single room school houses. They had moved a number of these school houses from the country into town adjacent to an elementary building. There was one kindergarten class per building and I believe there were five different kindergarten classes. I was born in 1947 and our class was very large, over 120 members, we were one of the first classes of "baby boomers". I don't remember a lot of specifics of kindergarten. We did attend class all day long. We started our basic learning process and did a little artsy craftsy stuff, which I was not very good at. We had our forced rest time every day after lunch, where we would lay a little rug on the wood floor and stretch out for 30-40 minutes. Because we lived in the country, we rode a school bus every day to and from school. This was a little scary at first. You certainly did not want to get on the wrong bus and not make it home at night. Those first few days of school, I can remember walking around with a big number pinned to my shirt, which corresponded to the bus I was supposed to ride home on. Kindergarten was that first big step of mingling and socializing with people you did not know. There were no organized pre-schools or day care centers at that time. We all survived and went on to first grade.

In Vinton, there were two elementary schools the East School and the West School and grades one through five in each school. The East School was located in the east part of town and most of the country kids attended this school along with the kids that lived on the east side of town. The West School was located in the west part of town and only kids that lived in the city attended that school. The East School was very old, built in the early 1900's, and was made of limestone. There were large wooden stair wells at each end of the building. They had a nice comfortable squeak as you went up and down. The halls seemed wide at the time with heavy wooden doors leading to each class room. The classrooms were bright and airy, large casement windows lined the outside walls that let in lots of natural sunlight. There was no air conditioning during that time. The rooms were heated in the winter with hot water radiators. There seemed to be no happy medium with them. The room was either like an oven or you shivered from the cold. Those radiators would clang and bang as the steam poured through them, you just knew someday they would explode. In the basement of the East School was the cafeteria. Everyday at noon, we would file down by classes to have our noon lunch. Some meals were great and then some were just plain awful. Everyone ate the same thing every day; there was not a smorgasbord of entrees, salads, and drinks to choose from. The meals I enjoyed the most were the days we had hot dogs, or mashed potatoes with hamburger gravy. I hated the days we had macaroni and cheese or egg salad sandwiches. To this day I can not eat egg salad sandwiches because of the ones we were served in grade school. I remember the kids across the table from me eating those sandwiches, they would talk with their mouths open and the egg salad would either fall out or be sticking to their teeth. It was nasty. I do not recall her name, but one of our teachers insisted we try a bite or two of anything that was on our plate. Some days I nearly gagged trying to choke down something I didn't like. I quickly learned to either stuff some of the food in a milk carton or throw some of it underneath the lunch table so it looked like I had tried some of the food. I think that is why I never really force my kids to eat anything, because I had that trick pulled on me when I was young.

I remember most of my grade school teachers. They were all women, but very dedicated to teaching the minds full of mush that entered their classrooms. Some were young, some were older, but all insisted on strict discipline. They also insisted that we learned our lessons. If a child failed to learn, they took it very personally. At this stage in my life, I am truly grateful to those teachers who instilled in me the desire to learn and the appreciation for a good education.

Some how, most of us survived elementary school and went on to Junior High, now called middle school. Junior high brought together the elementary kids from East School and West School. So, that meant there were lots of new faces and new friends to meet. Junior High also meant you no longer stayed in one classroom and had one teacher for the entire year. Each subject was taught by a different teacher and you moved to his or her classroom, they did not come to you. Another aspect of Junior High that was very common place in that era, but would probably be illegal today was class placement by ability. In other words, the top students were in one class for Science, Math, English, Geography, etc. There were about five different sections for each subject. This would probably seem unfair today, but it did allow a teacher to tailor each class to the abilities of their students. Unlike today where "mainstreaming" is the norm. My first year in Junior High, 6th grade, also meant I would have a man for a teacher, a new experience. This turned out to be no big deal. Our Junior High building was called Lincoln Junior High. It was the former High School in Vinton. The school system was expanding rapidly as the baby boomers started heading off to school. Once again, my teachers were excellent at what they did; they were dedicated professionals trying to pass on their knowledge to a reluctant bunch of youths.

One of the aspects of Junior High I enjoyed was "study hall". This was a very large room where you would come to work on some of your course work. There were 3-4 other classes in there at the same time. There was usually one teacher that monitored the activity and offered you some help if you needed it. Surprisingly, study hall was pretty quiet. Study hall gave you the opportunity to get your homework done without taking it home or relax a bit from the daily grind of class. Occasionally, a few side conversations would get started and the monitor would come break them up if they became too loud. It was also a great place to pass notes back and forth. You certainly did not want to get caught by the monitor. You were given a good tongue lashing and your notes were confiscated. That could be a little embarrassing depending on what you were writing on the notes. Our principal, Ernie Purcell, had his office next to the study hall area and he could peer out his window and survey the entire room. You certainly did not want Mr. Purcell catching you doing something wrong.

Ernie truly struck terror in the hearts of the Junior High students. He was a small, stocky man, with a butch hair cut. When Ernie got upset, his face turned a bright red and the veins on his forehead would bulge. There was no mistaken when he was mad. He ruled that junior high like a drill sergeant mans his troops. He spent a fair amount of time patrolling the halls looking for trouble makers. Ernie wanted control and order. There was to be no running, loud talking, or rude behavior in the halls at any time. God help the person who broke the rules. I can recall a number of times when he would take off in hot pursuit of a rule breaker, most of the time it was one of the boys. He would usually grab them by the shoulder and throw them up against the lockers. This was then followed by a verbal tirade and a trip to his office for more disciplinary action. I don't think Ernie would make it in this "hands off" world we have now in the school system. Needless to say there were very few problems in "Ernie's" world. This was also the era when if you got in trouble at school, you were in even deeper trouble when you got home. My parents were firm believers in a good education and strict discipline while you were in school. The principal and the teacher's word was the law, not some lame excuse you proposed as to why you got into trouble.

Junior High was also the first opportunity to participate in organized sports and organized school events such as after school dances. In a small rural town and during that time period, there were only a handful of sports activities; football, basketball, track, and baseball. I joined the football and basketball teams. I did not participate in track or baseball because they were spring and summer events and there was just too much to do on the farm to be participating in those activities. Junior High sports were a lot of fun, especially the bus trips to other towns to compete against someone other than your classmates or friends.

The Junior High dances were great fun too. They were called "sock hops". They were called that because the dances were held in the school gymnasium and you were not allowed on the gym floor with street shoes. So, you took off your shoes and danced around in your socks. I believe one or two teachers and one or two parents chaperoned those events. Their biggest job was not to keep law and order, but to encourage the guys to dance with the gals. The music came from a record player on the stage and the records came from students who brought their favorite "45's". The guys would sit in the bleachers and the gals would be on the gym floor dancing with each other. There was no D.J. but from time to time one of the chaperones would announce a "ladies choice" dance to pry a few guys out of the bleachers. This had to be a slow dance of course and once the dance was over, there was usually a mad dash back to reclaim your seat in the bleachers. I think you also need to understand this was a time when Rock 'n Roll was coming into its own. Icons such as Elvis, Chubby Checker, Little Richard and the like were just beginning to influence the dancing habits of America's youth. If you were going to dance "fast" i.e. the jitterbug, you probably needed a few lessons first. You could not just stand on the dance floor and flail about and make people think you were dancing. We had a few guys who were excellent fast and slow dancers and the rest of us clods were not about to hit the dance floor and embarrass ourselves. This was also a time when all the lights in the gym were on. When you danced, you better have your hands above your partner's waist; no butt squeezing back then.

It was very evident at the school dances, but also in the day to day activities of Junior High students that the gals were maturing physically ahead of the guys. Those flat chested girls were beginning to show some curves and most of them had taken their growth spurts and were now taller than most of the boys. Conversations amongst the guys centered more and more on the opposite sex and who might be natural and who might be using some upper body enhancements.

There were also dress codes back then. Girls could wear skirts and blouses, and dresses, but no shorts or slacks, even in the winter. The skirts needed to reach the knees or lower. The boys were to wear shirts, tucked into their pants. All pants required a belt. Everyone had to be well groomed, no wild hair dos or hair colors allowed. Anyone not complying with the dress code found themselves in the principal's office and if you violated the code too often, you were suspended from school, no questions asked.

Those three years in Junior High passed rather quickly. However, what seemed fun and exciting only three short years ago was now becoming mundane and boring; it was time to move on to the big times, High School. Vinton's High School was named after our first president, Washington. Heading to high school was really scary. You went from being the mighty eighth grader to the lowly freshman. My older sister was in high school then and I really did not relish the idea of her keeping an eye on me. She was also an excellent student and my high school teachers were continually reminding me of that fact. She had set the bar just a little too high for me.

Just as Junior High presented many more activities than grade school, high school offered even more things to do. You could begin to choose courses you wanted to take as opposed to everyone taking the same thing. Because I wanted to go to college, I centered on Math, Science, and foreign languages. Once again, my teachers were dedicated professionals. A couple of teachers were not necessarily the best at teaching, but you had no doubt that their hearts were in the right place. Much of what was present in Junior High; discipline, dress codes, etc. was carried over into High School. School was a place to learn and grow, it was not a place to raise hell and be disrespectful to those in authority or your fellow classmates.

I could probably look at the teachers in my high school year book and tell a story or two of what went on in their class, but it would take volumes to do that. Most of my classes were interesting and challenging. I was never a very avid reader so literature classes were not my favorite. On the other hand, my innate curiosity about things and what made them work made classes like biology and chemistry very interesting. As with most people, the academics became secondary to the interactions you had with your fellow classmates. All of the activities you did together in school and out of school developed very strong friendships that have a way of enduring for a long time. These interactions and experiences become obvious at our class reunions. It just takes one or two "hey do you remember the time we did this or that" and the memories of those days come rushing back. My fondest memories were playing high school football and the bonds that were formed with your fellow team mates. I also remember our class as a group of people who enjoyed each other, both male and female. There was some dating and even some couples going steady. For the most part, however, we seemed to do a lot of fun things together and did not always have to be paired up.

Probably the biggest event of the school year was the Junior/Senior Prom. As the event implied this was a big event for the juniors and seniors only, unless you were invited by a junior or senior to be their date for the night. The prom was held in the high school gymnasium. It was the responsibility of the Junior Class to put on the prom for the senior class. The juniors had to pick a prom theme. The gym was decorated according to the overall theme. The evening started with a dinner, served in the gym. The mothers of the junior students would prepare the meal in the high school cafeteria. A few select sophomores were picked to be the waiters and waitresses for the meal. The guys would wear a nice sport coat and tie. The gals of course would pick out their "prom" dress. You would need to get them a corsage for their dress and they would get you a boutonnière for your sport coat. That was pretty much the expense for the evening. You certainly did not rent an expensive tuxedo or go to a fancy restaurant for dinner. Everyone could afford to go and it was pretty much expected everyone would go to the prom, date or not. After the dinner, the tables were pushed back a bit to make a dance floor. The music was provided by a live local band. The prom and the homecoming dance were the only dances with live music; at the rest of the high school dances music was provided by a record player. After the dance, the local theatre would have a movie or two to watch for just the prom attendees. Things began to wind down around two or three in the morning. Many would call it a night at this point, while others would adjourn to a home for breakfast, or to the woods to have a beer or two. It was a wonderful night to say the least. The dinner, the dance, the movie afterwards, staying up late; this only happened once a year and it was something you looked forward to and remember a long time.

Getting a date for the prom was a big deal and you started this process months before the big event, usually held in early May. As a freshman and sophomore boy, you had little or no chance of going to the prom; junior and senior girls rarely invited underclassman to the prom. However, junior and senior guys would often times invite underclassman to the prom. So, when you were a junior or senior, you had the pickings of four different classes of women. When I was a junior, I committed the unspeakable sin of inviting a girl from another town, actually a gal I had met at 4-H camp. When I was a senior, I was dating a fellow classmate and the decision was easy. My mom had to field a whole bunch of phone calls my senior year. It seems the mothers of the senior girls who had no dates felt it was the obligation of the senior boys to make sure all the senior girls had dates for the prom. They seemed to forget that many of them went as freshman and sophomores and us guys spent prom night hanging out somewhere. Fortunately, prom night fell toward the end of the school year and this became a mute issue once we all graduated.

I mentioned in one of the other chapters about what a big deal "Friday nights" were in small town rural Iowa. In the fall, high school football games were a very big deal. If you happened to live in one of those towns where football was "king", it was a very big deal indeed. Although football was popular in Vinton, we were not known to be a football powerhouse; actually we were quite the opposite. This was in part due to an unfortunate accident where a young man suffered a broken neck on the playing field and was paralyzed. Somehow, the town just never got over that tragedy. Any way "football Friday nights" were a lot of fun. It was a good time to come out on Friday night after a long week. The fall weather in Iowa could be quite brisk and crisp and very refreshing. It was a good place for all the school kids to meet and blow off a little steam. The town's people liked to come out and support the team and of course you could always count on the parents of the players to be there. There was certainly a lot of arm chair quarterbacking in the stands. The high school band was always there as well to pump up the crowd and perform at half time. When I was in Junior High that was the place to be on Friday nights. Junior High students were relegated to a certain section of the bleachers. One or two teachers were in charge of keeping us reasonably under control. I can't say that we paid a whole lot of attention to the game, but we sure had a great time in the stands. When I was in High School, I played on the football team. I was quite small as a freshman and sophomore, but still played a lot. I took a spurt of growth between my sophomore year and junior year and looked a little bit more like a football player my senior year. It was especially fun to be out on the field on Friday nights and having all the people cheering you on. Our first game my senior year was against Belle Plaine. They were expected to have a really good team that year and they kept telling us how they were just going to pummel us on the field. The game was in Belle Plaine and we won the game rather decidedly. It was a great feeling since we truly were the under dogs and we were able to win that big game. Later on in the season, a bone in my hand was broken in a game and I could not play the rest of the year. I was very disappointed to say the least. It was pretty cool in school the week after the Friday night game, particularly if you had a few scraps and bruises. The girls would want to know how you got them during the game.

Although not as big a deal as the Junior/Senior Prom, Homecoming was a pretty big school event as well. Each class designed and built a float for the Homecoming parade. The football players would usually pile into some big truck and ride through the parade as well. A few of the school clubs and one or two businesses would also build a float. These were just old farm hay wagons decorated with painted cardboard and streamers. To make the parade complete, the Homecoming queen and each of her attendants would ride in a convertible with the top down. The parade could not have lasted more than 15 minutes as it wound up and down the downtown streets. That seemed like a real big deal back then, but seems a little hokey now.

There was also a Homecoming Dance after the football game on Friday night. If you played in the game, you had to hustle to get cleaned up and then go to the dance. You might wear a sport coat and tie for the dance, certainly not the formality that you see with Homecoming Dances today. We did have a live band for Homecoming as well. It was not a real big deal if you did not have a date, but it was a lot more fun if you did. Anyone in high school could attend the dance and anyone who was an alumnus of the school could also attend. I don't recall a whole lot of alumni coming to the dance; it was just not a real cool thing to do. I had just started going steady with one of my classmates at that time and this turned out be a major first date.

As I mentioned earlier the friends and the good times were a big part of high school. Hanging out at the local diners, going to the movies together, driving around town, playing sports, often times just sitting around talking about life, made the high school experience truly unique.

A conversation about school would not be complete without talking about graduation day. Just as junior high became routine and mundane, high school seemed to be following the same path. I think most everyone in our class looked forward to that day when we got that diploma and headed off for bigger and better things. I do not remember the day of the week we had graduation, I think it was a Friday, but I know it was in the evening. Like so many high school events, graduation was held in the high school gym. Chairs were placed on the gym floor for the graduates and their immediate families sat behind them. The bleachers behind the chairs were for other relatives and friends of the family. Everyone faced the stage. The stage had a podium; chairs for the school board, school dignitaries, and commencement speaker; some flowers; and the American and Iowa Flag. It was a very warm May evening and it was very warm underneath our cap and gowns. I don't remember one word of the commencement address, but I am sure the advice was very profound. I do remember receiving my diploma from my dad however. Dad was on the local school board at that time. It was the custom that if you were on the board and you had a son or daughter graduating you got to hand out the diplomas with the superintendent. I was proud and honored to receive my diploma that night from dad. After the ceremony, we adjourned to our farm house for a little graduation party. Many of my aunts and uncles were there as they all lived so close. I remember opening the graduation cards and gifts. I enjoyed the cash and checks the most as I knew I would need that money as I headed off to college in a few months. It was not a wild celebration, just punch, ice cream, and cake with family quietly celebrating one of life's milestones. This was very typical of how these events were celebrated. They had been repeated many times before with my older cousins and would be repeated again as my younger cousins graduated as well.

Unique Farm Activities

There were many activities that took place almost daily on the farm, morning and evening chores, tending the livestock, and tending the crops. A few activities that were rather unique to the farm scene occurred only once or twice a year.

Homemade Sausage

One such activity was making homemade sausage. On our farm, we raised pigs, milked cows, and had feeder cattle. Periodically, dad would take a pig or steer to the local "meat locker" to be butchered. The local butcher would process the meat and then wrap it in white butcher paper. We would then bring that meat home and store it in our freezer along with other frozen meats, fruits, and vegetables. At least once or twice a year, dad would have the butcher grind up some beef and some pork and blend the two together to make sausage. He would haul home these ground meats in large tubs. Once home, he and mom would mix in salt, pepper, garlic, and a variety of other spices to make the sausage. Mom would then cook up some of this mixture to make sure it had the proper flavor. When it was just right, it was then O.K. to actually make it into sausage.

We had a large, cast iron sausage press. It was a large black cylindrical device. You filled the chamber with the blended meat and spices. A large flat plate was then slowly cranked down onto the meat. This forced the meat out a tube in the bottom of the sausage press. The meat was forced into natural sausage casings, i.e. intestines. Each sausage was about two feet long. The casings were cut, the ends twisted and then tied tightly closed with butcher cord. The sausages were then hung on boards in the basement. I can't really recall just how many sausages we made at a time, but I am sure there were at least 50-60 of these two foot long sausages when we got done processing all of that meat. The sausages would hang in the basement over night. The next day we would haul all of those sausages back to the local locker. The butcher would wrap a few of them up in the white paper. However, most of the sausage would be naturally slow smoked over the next two days. You could always tell when meats were being smoked at the local locker. There was this very delightful smell that emanated from this small butcher plant for two to three days while the process was going on. Once the sausages were smoked, the butcher would wrap them up, freeze them, and then send them home to our freezer. There was nothing quite like that home made, slow smoked sausage. It was always a treat, no matter whether it was for breakfast, dinner, or supper. We were one of the few families that actually made their own sausage. Our friends and neighbors always enjoyed receiving them as mom would occasionally give them away, as just being neighborly.

Butchering Chickens

I mentioned earlier that mom always got several hundred baby chicks every spring. She would get about 100 roosters and 300 pullets, which became the laying hens. When the roosters were large enough, they would be butchered and put in our freezer. The butchering process would start the night before. These young roosters would not go back in the chicken coop at night, but would roost in the hardwood trees of our small grove. It would have been nearly impossible to catch them during the day, but at night while they were roosting, they were easy picking's. When it was dark, we would head back into the woods to catch them. We would use a small ladder and flashlights to spot them in the trees. We would only want the roosters, so we would have to sort through all the chickens on the tree limbs and only pull the roosters out of the tree. We would then put them in chicken coops to await their fate in the morning. Butchering the roosters was pretty much Mom's job along with my sisters. From time to time some of the neighborhood ladies would be over if they were going to take some of the roosters home to their freezers. This was always quite a project.

The roosters were plucked from their coop and suspended upside down on the clothes line. Baling twine was placed on the clothes line and then slipped over their feet. When there were a half dozen roosters hanging upside down on the clothes line, mom would cut off their heads with a butcher knife. Once beheaded, the roosters would flap their wings like crazy and bleed profusely from their severed neck. Shortly, they were dead. Every now and then, one of the beheaded roosters would break loose from the twine and hit the ground. It would flail about aimlessly for a few seconds, but it too would be gone. Once these birds were dead, it was time to start the actual butchering process. The birds were first dipped in very hot water. This was to loosen the feathers. The feathers were then plucked from the birds. Despite everyone's best efforts, a few pin feathers remained. These were easily removed by holding each bird over a small open fire, usually burning newspaper, to singe off those pesky remaining feathers. After the feathers were removed, the lower scaly part of the legs were cut off, leaving a nice clean looking carcass. The real tricky work still remained. The carcass was slit open with a large knife and the internal organs were removed. Certain internal organs were delicacies, i.e. the heart, liver, and gizzard, and had to be separated from the other organs and preserved. Once this process was completed the bird was thoroughly washed inside and out with hot water. Mom would wrap up a few whole birds and freeze them. Most of the roosters, however, she would carve up into legs, thighs, wings, and breasts and freeze them. Mom did not bake whole chickens often, but loved to bread the individual pieces and fry them in her electric fry pan. Her fried chicken was delicious. Butchering 20-25 roosters at a time was usually a full morning's job from start to finish. It was a lot of work, but being able to have fried chicken during the winter months was a very good thing.

Trapping Gophers

If you ever watched the movie "Caddy Shack" with Rodney Dangerfield, you found out just how pesky gophers can be to a golf course. Gophers or pocket gophers as we called them on the farm could also wreak havoc in the hay fields or grazing pastures. You could easily spot where gophers were doing their dirty work. They would borrow through the ground feeding on the roots of the hay and pastures plants. Periodically, they would borrow a hole up to the surface and push all the dirt from their newly formed tunnels into a large mound of dirt or a "gopher mound". Not only were they destroying the plants, but these large mounds of dirt looked unsightly in the pasture; made the tractor bounce as you drove over them, or jammed up the sickle blade of the hay mower. Although they did not create a huge financial loss, they were a nuisance and dad did not like the sight of gopher mounds in his hay fields and pastures. He did not like the damage they did to his hay mowers as well. The easy way to do them in was to put some poison impregnated peanuts or potatoes in one of their tunnels. The gophers would eat them and would assume ground temperature shortly after consuming the poisoned food.

Although this was an efficient way of getting rid of the gophers, you did not really realize you had done the gopher in until new gopher mounds stopped appearing in the fields. There was another way and this was actually a cash generating scheme. You see, gophers were looked at as vermin in the rural counties of Iowa. You received a 5 cent bounty on every pair of gopher's feet you brought in. So, that meant you had to trap them and bring in the front feet of the gopher in order to receive your bounty.

Trapping gophers required a certain amount of skill, a little bit of work, and a great deal of patience. It was a skill passed down through the family. My older brother learned it from dad and my brother then taught me how to trap these little varmints. Gophers are nocturnal and do not see very well. So, if you wanted to be a successful trapper, you needed to get up early in the morning and go out into the fields where the gopher mounds were. You needed to find a "fresh" mound, i.e. one where the soil had just been freshly dug and pushed to the surface. You pushed away the fresh soil until you found the tunnel opening. The opening led down into the soil where it formed a "T" with the connecting tunnels. This is where you placed the jaws of the steel trap, hoping the nearly blind gopher would wander across the trap and be caught. After the trap was in place, you would place a thin flat board over the hole; we used an old cedar shingle, and then pushed the soil on top of the board to seal the opening. The trap had a chain attached to it which was then looped over a stake in the ground so the gopher could not drag the trap away. If there were several fresh mounds in one area, you might place two or three traps. Most of the time however, you would go to another area of the field where another set of gopher mounds had appeared and repeat the trapping process.

If you felt ambitious, you would return to the field in the evening to see if you had caught anything. Most gophers remained fairly quiet during the day and it would be a rare event to catch one during the day. You did however; return the next morning to see if you had out-smarted Mr. Gopher. As you approached the mounds, you generally had a good idea if your trapping efforts had been successful. Good signs were no fresh mounds or the mound where you had set your trap was disturbed, occasionally the gopher would be on top of the ground in the trap. If there was a fresh mound of soil or your trapping area looked the same as you left it, you could bet your efforts had failed. Irregardless, you would push away the soil and see if you had a gopher in the trap. If you caught a gopher, most of the time it would be in the trap and dead. Sometimes, the gopher was still alive and you would have to drag it out of the hole and whack it over the head to kill it. The really clever gophers would push soil ahead of them and spring the trap, or just totally avoid the tunnel with the trap in it. If you had caught a gopher, you might still reset the trap in case there was another gopher in the area. If you failed in your efforts, you would look for a fresh mound and redo the trapping process. You would then proceed to the next trapping bed and see if your efforts paid off there.

As I said earlier, you received a bounty of 5 cents for every pair of gopher's feet you brought it. You would bring home the dead gophers and then cut off there front feet. The feet were then placed in a bottle with lots of salt that supposedly kept the feet from deteriorating. Periodically, you would take your jar of gopher's feet into the court house to collect your bounty. I believe you had to take your jar of gopher feet to the auditor first. I am sure this was one of their favorite tasks. They would pour the concoction of salt and gopher feet on a piece of wax paper and carefully count the pairs of feet. Once the feet were counted, the auditor would fill out a voucher and you would then take that to the county treasurer to collect your bounty. Ten pairs of feet equaled 50 cents. Not a pile of cash, but that 50 cents would buy 10 nickel candy bars or 5 ice cream sandwiches or a burger and drink at Cronk's café. Life was good.

Mom's Cooking Talents

I would probably be remiss if I did not mention some of the unique things my mom did with her cooking talents. She was an excellent cook and part of what made her cooking so special was her ability to create things from the raw ingredients rather than buy them made up in a can or box at the grocery store.

One such example of this was her home made egg noodles. She would blend flour and eggs together to make the noodle "dough". She would then take a rolling pin and press the dough into large thin sheets that resembled large very thin pizza crusts. These sheets of noodles had to air dry to a certain texture before they could be cut into noodles. When the time was right, she would stack several of these sheets together and hand cut them into noodles. She always made a bunch of them, so she would put them in plastic bags and what she felt would not be used right away would go in the freezer. Her noodles were terrific by themselves, but made the best chicken noodle soup. Even as an adult, I always encouraged mom to bring some of her noodles when she paid us a visit.

Homemade sauerkraut was another specialty of mom. Mom would harvest several heads of cabbage from the garden, pull off a few coarse outer leaves, and give each head a thorough cleaning. She then would shred each head on a large shredding board making large mounds of shredded cabbage. She would then stuff the shredded cabbage into large fruit jars. Mom prepared a brine solution and would fill the jars with this solution. She would place a screw top lid on each jar, but not tighten it down. I am not sure how long it took, but she would let the jars ferment for several days, converting shredded cabbage into sauerkraut. Once again, when the time was right she would seal the jars of sauerkraut and store them away in her fruit cellar.

A similar process was making pickles. Mom made at least three varieties of pickles; dills, sweet, and bread and butter pickles. Each one had its own recipe, which I could not even begin to know. Mom would harvest lots of cucumbers. Some we would eat fresh as cucumber salad or just plain. The rest would be made into pickles. Mom would sort them out, usually the large ones would be made into dills, the smaller ones into sweet pickles, and others would be sliced and made into bread and butter pickles. Each variety was stuffed into canning jars and the appropriate pickling solution poured in to the top. Mom used to grow her own "dill" which made her dill pickles really good. The jars would ferment for a few days and then be sealed and stored away in the fruit cellar along with the rest of the garden harvest.

I have mentioned many times about mom's ability to make the best pies and cakes. Once again, these were all made from scratch, no box mixes for her. Mom also made homemade rolls, doughnuts, and pastries. Once in a while, she would make actual loaves of bread, but she preferred more of the specialty items. She would combine the flour, yeast, sugar, etc. to make the dough. The dough was allowed to rise before she would make her creations. The smell of fresh dough rising was always great and us kids would love to eat the fresh dough before it was baked. Mom would then take the dough and create dinner rolls, cinnamon rolls, or doughnuts. The doughnuts were deep fat fried in lard and then covered with a white icing. The cinnamon rolls were also covered with a white icing. The house always smelled so good when these items were baking. Nothing smelled better than to come in from chores in the morning during winter and have mom's cinnamon rolls warming in the oven for breakfast. The smells were great, but to eat them was even better, her creations would literally melt in your mouth.

Gene & Verna with Farm Kitten

Verna with puppies -1949

Gene with a puppy

Jo & Lu with orphan lamb in house basement

Childhood Pets

When you are born and raised on a farm, you are exposed to a variety of animals on a daily basis. You get to see animals born frequently and you get to see a ton of baby animals such as calves, pigs, lambs, chicks, ducklings, guineas, puppies and kittens. You are able to watch them grow up to adults in a very short period of time. Because you are so close to nature, you also are privileged to see a variety of "wild" animals as well such as rabbits, squirrels, raccoons, opossums, foxes, and a myriad of birds including pheasants, migratory birds, predatory birds, and the less desirables such as pigeons and sparrows. Raising livestock was an important income stream so taking good care of them was a must. That might include help a sow deliver her pigs, a cow deliver her calf, or a ewe deliver her lamb. Once they were born, you might have to give additional support to the newborn in terms of hand feeding or bottle feeding. This was particularly true of baby lambs and calves. Newborn dairy calves would be allowed to nurse their mothers for a few days, but were then switched to milk replacer so their mother's milk could be sold. That was always a fun job to do. These dairy calves would be in a pen off the milking area and they would go crazy when you would come in, because they knew they would soon get a meal. From time to time an orphaned lamb would also be in with the dairy calves. Some of these lambs would believe they were cattle rather than sheep as they grew up. You would often times see them in the pasture with the dairy cows, rather than the sheep.

As I said earlier, on a livestock farm you raised animals to be sold to contribute to the farm income. You quickly learned not to get too attached because at some point these animals would be sold. Female dairy calves, heifers, were somewhat different; because you would often times keep a good dairy heifer and raise her to be a full fledged milk cow, which could be on the farm for several years. Lambs were by far the cutest of the baby animals and they were especially fun if you got to bottle feed them. However, they never seemed to be too affectionate and grew up to be smelly adult sheep.

There were always lots of cats around as well. These were rarely considered as pets however. On a farm, they had a definite purpose, keep the rat and mice population to a minimum. These farm cats truly demonstrated the principle of "survival of the fittest". They were not given any commercial cat food; they survived on what they were able to catch. They were not vaccinated for any disease and if they were injured, they either healed themselves or succumbed to their problem. I recall one mother cat that probably raised 10 litters of kittens. She had most of one of her rear legs cut off by a hay mower. That did not deter her hunting abilities however. She could catch wild rabbits, squirrels and rats and mice were no match for her hunting talents. That old mother cat proved to me just how tough a farm cat was and what many would see as a mobility handicap, didn't matter at all to her. As I said before, there was no veterinary care extended to these cats. Many succumbed to distemper, respiratory disease, automobiles, and various and assorted other farm accidents. An old farm cat might be three years old. Anything older than that was a very savvy cat. The cats that hung out in the dairy barn were afforded the luxury of fresh milk morning and night. They also enjoyed the warmth of those large dairy cows in the winter. Their biggest hazard was being kicked or stepped on by one of the cows.

Every farm seemed to have at least one dog and some might have two or three. These were mostly mixed breed mongrels that were dumped in the country or maybe some neighbor's female dog had a litter of pups and felt you deserved one of them. Most of these farm dogs served no real useful purpose. They usually just hung out on the farmstead and would bark whenever a car or truck pulled on the yard. Every now and then you would get a dog that you could train to herd cattle, kill rats that were infesting your granaries, or be a good guard dog to protect the property. They did not receive a lot of veterinary care either. You might do a little something for them if they had some useful trait. Many succumbed to disease, cars, or farm accidents just like the cats.

I can't recall how many dogs we had, but three of them stick out in my mind. One was a large mixed breed dog named Shep that loved to hunt raccoons. In the summer, he would wait until dark and then patrol one of the two creeks that ran through our farm. Raccoons are typically nocturnal and would frequent the creeks at night to look for fish or wash their evening meal. I only witnessed his hunting expertise on a couple of occasions. Shep would usually walk the creek beds and when he found a raccoon, he would engage it in a fight to the death. Raccoons were incredibly tough and when challenged would put up a very vigorous fight. The larger the raccoon, the bigger and the longer the fight. To my knowledge, he always won and no raccoon ever escaped his death grip. After the raccoon was dead, Shep would proceed to drag it back to the farmstead and lay it next to mom's garden. This was no small task in light of the fact some raccoons weighed over 30 pounds and our farmstead was a good ¼ to ½ mile from the creeks. Mom was not overly thrilled with this, but Shep seemed extremely proud of his accomplishment.

Shep never chased or threatened any of the neighbors' livestock. Our neighbor Bill, who raised sheep, was convinced our dog was going to chase and kill some of his sheep. He had talked to dad about this, but dad did not seem overly concerned and we did not confine him to the yard. Bill told dad he might get a Billy goat to run with the sheep. It was a common practice then to have a large Billy goat with the sheep to protect them from dogs that might bother or chase the sheep. Not long after his last conversation with dad, a very large Billy goat with very large horns was in the pasture with the Bill's sheep. Not long after that, dad and I were coming back from town. We could see Shep dragging something up the road just a few yards from the entrance to the farmstead. Yes, old Shep had visited the neighbor's sheep herd and killed the Billy goat. As with the raccoons, he was proud of his kill and brought it home to show all of us. That was a huge Billy goat as well, he probably weighed 80 pounds. That did not matter to Shep. He had a hold of one of his horns and was proudly dragging it home to the farm. Dad did not know whether to curse or laugh, but we both decided to laugh. He called Bill and told him of the demise of his goat. The following week, dad went to the sale barn and picked up another Billy goat for Bill. They were very cheap, probably cost dad less than $10. Strangely, Shep never went back there. I guess he just wanted to make his point.

Another dog I remember well was Mike or Moochie. For some reason that dog really liked me and would follow me any where I went. If I went into the barn, he followed. He would go up in the hay mow and scale the bales of hay like a mountain goat. If I got into a farm wagon, he had to be there as well. He could take a running jump and get into the wagon. He learned to herd cattle and would help me round up the dairy cattle from the pasture. He never came in the house though and slept in my room. That was definitely a rule that was never broken. Dogs were outside animals and they did not come into the house. I could certainly count on him waiting at the back door in the morning when I came out to do the morning chores. He was certainly the closest pet I ever had on the farm. Unfortunately, I caused his demise. One summer day I was mowing some pasture and as always, he had to be out there with me. For some unknown reason, he darted in front of the mower and before I could stop, the mower cut off two of his legs. Dad was not far away and came running because Moochie was whaling in pain. Dad and I walked up to the house. We talked it over and decided that he was suffering and because two of his legs were gone, it would be best if Moochie were put down. I think dad was as upset as I was because Moochie was such a loveable dog.

He told me to stay at the house. He took the rifle off the shelf and ended Moochie's suffering. I don't think I had undergone anything that emotionally traumatic before. It took me a long time to get over Moochie as he was such a good friend and pet.

The other dog I would like to talk about was Lassie. She was a purebred collie. I think this was the only purebred dog we ever owned. The folks got her from friends. I was in high school when we got her so, I did not spend much time with her. She was an excellent livestock dog and an excellent specimen of the collie breed. I think she was one of the few dogs that received veterinary care as well.

Besides the usually run of regular pets, I also had a few other critters as well. We found a baby raccoon once that we kept for a while. Her name was Cindy. Like most wild animals, she was cute and good, but as she got older, her wild tendencies began to show. She was eventually released to the wild. I also raised some foxes, but they never seemed to show any calm tendencies and they too were released back into the wild. My brother and I would also catch some pigeons that would roost in the barn and put them in an old chicken coop. I believe at one time we had as many as 8 pigeons. These birds never seemed to tame down and became about as much work as mom's chickens. They were allowed to fly free around the farm.

As you can see, I was very fortunate to have a variety of animals during my childhood. I probably didn't realize just how fortunate I was until I became more of an urban dweller and not have the opportunity to have so many animals around. Animals certainly provide a vital connection between us and the environment.

About the Author

The author is a veterinarian with over 33 years of experience. He was born in 1947, a true baby boomer, and spent the first 18 years of his life on an Iowa farm. You will appreciate his easy writing style and subtle humor as he describes the day to day events of the time. His description of people, places, and events, makes his book an easy read and will create a desire to return time and again to reread the heart warming stories.

www.ingramcontent.com/pod-product-compliance
Lightning Source LLC
Chambersburg PA
CBHW061402280526
45784CB00001B/340